OUR JOURNEY OF GOD'S BLESSINGS

A Special Needs Family Remembers

Arie Gray

**Northumberland
Historical Press**
NHP

Northumberland Historical Press
Heathsville, Virginia

Author Contact Information:
Linkedin: Linkedin.com/in/arie-gray-b4b707148
Email: SpecialNeedsRevival@gmail.com
Facebook: Arie Gray Author

ISBN: 978-1-957928-36-4
Library of Congress Control Number: 2023905788

Printed in the United States of America

This book is dedicated to the memory of our parents Lawrence & Bertha Johnson, Rev. C.C. & Pauline Gray, and our mentor, Rev. Dr. T.W. Morris

It is also dedicated to *all* of you who read this book as you travel on your journey. Blessings to you all!

ACKNOWLEDGEMENTS

I must begin by thanking God for blessing me and bringing to my remembrance His many acts of love! His "urging" led me to author this book. To our brothers and sisters, you all have been a part of our journey. Aunt Woncey, thanks for being a mom to us. To my Uncle George and Aunt Barbara, you are an inspiration. Thanks to all of those who have prayed for us, especially family, Godparents, and friends. To my Hampton friends i.e., Vicky, Lafonda, Kim, and Kitty, your fortitude has always encouraged me.

God truly blessed us with the wonderful church families from Sargent Memorial Presbyterian Church and First Baptist Church of Merrifield. To Marilyn & the Sargent Gospel-Aires and Spirit of Truth Christian Church, much love! Joanne, thanks for everything, including you developing Jasmine and Jessica's praise dancing capabilities. To all of my music teachers and musicians, including Dr. Roland Carter, Dr. Shelia Maye, Ivan & William Brown and former Ambition Band members, thanks for cultivating my musical growth. It enhanced my music ministry which helped me to remain "grounded" during the most challenging times of this journey.

There are so many people who have helped to inspire all three of our children. Kudos to the Ivymount School! To our daughters' Ivymount friends and their parents, YOU ARE AWESOME! Thank you, Jackie Zamora & Zamdance, and the Silver Hill Strikers Bowling League, as you developed our daughters into tournament winning bowlers. To the Best Buddies Organization, especially Alice Felker and Kendall Kaiser, thanks so much for your dedication to special needs youth!

Thanks to our many wonderful neighbors, including Reverends Larry & Lavern Finch, and the Martins, who have looked out for our children over the years. To Fairfield Knolls' neighbors, especially the Daleys and Bradleys, thanks so much for looking out for Dad. Wayne and Debbie, what a joy and support it was to have you as family, years ago, living 5 minutes from us!

To my DIA family, including prayer partners Rev. Sherita Seawright, Beverly Lee, Minister Lisa Purvis, Gayle Murchison, and Ron Woodward, I thank you all! Debbie and Paul Sell, you exampled how to be an advocate for special needs children. Warner, you are among those who are friends for life!

To our county's school bus drivers and assistants, including Ms. Kim and Ms. Darlene, you truly blessed our lives! To those Metro Access drivers such as Ms. Kimberly, who currently transport our daughters (especially those during the pandemic), and employees i.e. Ms. Eular, and Mr. Martin, we appreciate your dedication! To our daughters' Service Source supervisors, thanks for all you do.

To my brother, Dr. Larry Johnson, thanks for the many years of medical advice and assistance. Also, many thanks to medical personnel and staff, especially Medstar Health, who have taken care of us, especially during the pandemic. Special thanks to Dr. Helen Norwood, Dr. Geoffrey Sabloff, Dr. Vestinia Bridges, Medstar Medical Group Women's Health at Clinton and Medstar Health Radiology at Brandywine (i.e. Bill). Thanks also to Dr. Earl Armstrong, Dr. Herman Gist, Dr. James Chesley, Dr. Lornette Mills, Dr. Larry Hotchkiss, Dr. Arthur Barletta (National Spine & Pain Center), Dr. Warren Yu, Advanced Dermatology, Asthma, Allergy & Sinus Center, Dr. Edward Brown, Dr. Ernie Banks, Dr. Larry Bryant, and Sports Pro Physical Therapy. To Dr. Aakanksha Asija and her staff in North Carolina, words of thanks will never express our gratitude! To our local pharmacy, as well as everyone who worked during the pandemic to supply our needs, we are forever grateful!

Debbie Stevens, many thanks for taking wonderful care of our hair, especially during the pandemic! Special thanks to Les Henig Photography (cover photo) and Ameera's Images (bio photo). I'm grateful to Jan Beckett for her work with this project. Thanks to my cousin Gregory and all who encouraged me to write this book. Tommy, Carolyn, and Sheila, I appreciated your input.

To Geoffrey, Jasmine and Jessica, you mean more to me than you can ever know. I am so grateful that I am your mother and my love for each of you is forever. Geoffrey, you will help to inspire others who will experience your journey. God will be glorified! Finally, to my awesome and incredible husband, Charles Gray.... I love you so much and always will! Besides the Lord, you continue to be my rock and I am so grateful to you for everything!! God has blessed me with your faith, your strength, and your love for me and our special family! Thanks for traveling this journey with me!!

PREFACE

Remember when we were children, how we used to tease our classmates? Some of the things we said were funny, but some were rather crude. I remember kids insulting other kids, joking about them riding the "little yellow school bus." Everyone would laugh, including me. Little did we know what the future would bring and that some of us would someday see our own children riding a "little yellow school bus."

In my elementary school in St. Louis, Missouri, children with disabilities were not "mainstreamed," as is now the case in most school settings. Mainstreaming simply means placing children with disabilities in classrooms alongside children who do not need special assistance. Years ago, most, if not all, Special Education students had their own classrooms and teachers. But there was one student in my class who *did* have a disability. Her name was Sabrina, and she had polio. She wore knee braces and used crutches. Sabrina became my best friend. She was fun to be around, had a wonderful smile, and did not let her health stop her from excelling in school. I was blessed to be her friend, and we got along very well. When I was in the 8th grade, my family left Missouri. Although we lost touch with one another, I never forgot her, her sense of humor, and her strength.

Decades later, I now "wear the shoes" of Sabrina's mother and so many others. The journey of being a special needs parent has been the most challenging aspect of my life. In 1994, my husband and I embarked on this journey, one that we did not choose, had not planned for, nor were prepared for. It has been difficult, emotional, stressful, and at times, overwhelming. Neither friends nor family have truly understood what daily life has been like. Why? Because they don't live with us, and they don't experience what we do. They don't "wear the shoes," and their journey is different than ours or yours. Also, having two children with "special needs" may have been even more challenging than would be the case with one special needs child. However, there are so many other parents who have more challenges than we have experienced, and they are indeed very special people!

There are three purposes of this book. The first is to glorify God, which is to honor and praise Him, as He has sustained us during this entire journey. The second purpose is to reveal some of the blessings we have experienced that not only confirm that God is real, but that He loves us so very much. What are these blessings? I would describe "blessings" as acts that give happiness, protection, benefits or favor from a higher power, God. The third purpose is to encourage all of you on this journey called "Life." If you are the parents or guardians of special needs children, your journey may be very similar to ours. I hope that all the parents and guardians of "special children" who read this book will be encouraged to continue to believe in their children, their gifts, their talents, and their capabilities. But most of all, realize that we have a loving heavenly Father, who will help you on this special journey.

You may not "wear the shoes" of a special needs parent or guardian, so your journey may be different. However, your life may be just as challenging. You may be dealing with children or family members struggling with serious issues (e.g., drug abuse, sexual immorality, or criminality, etc.). Or you may have become a caregiver to an ailing spouse, parent or family member. You may be living with a physical illness or have undergone other life-changing circumstances.

Surviving these journeys produces a testimony, the very fact that you survived. We all have a testimony, which is our lifetime of experiences growing day by day. May your journey, and your testimony, include God's blessings along the way!

CONTENTS

Chapter 1

THE WEDDING DAY

I couldn't believe I was getting married, again! Thirty-nine years old, divorced with my five-year-old son Geoffrey, I had finally adjusted to heading a single-parent home. Life had not been easy, but we had survived. I also had wonderful, loving parents, who helped me in so many ways. I had decided that if I ever got married again, it would have to be obvious that God was in control. In fact, during the legal separation and ultimate divorce, I deliberately wore a ring on my left ring finger, so that if any man even thought to approach me, he hopefully would see my ring and leave me alone! Later, Charles Gray, who would become my boyfriend, referred to it as my "get back Jack ring." Anyway, I always felt that if I ever *did* marry again, the man would have to love God first and me second. Those were the conditions I prayed for.

Well, it happened, and here I was preparing to get married at my parents' home on February 5,1994. It was a cold but gorgeous day; the sun shone brightly, and the sky was a glorious shade of blue. It was a day I will never forget. Charles was like a prince charming and soul mate, all rolled up into a handsome, wonderful man. We had so much in common. We were both church musicians, who played the piano as well as other instruments, and sang. He loved the Lord and we had grown to deeply love each other. Another blessing was that he and Geoffrey got along very well. In fact, one day while we were still dating, Geoffrey told me that he wanted Charles and me to get married and have a daughter. He even wanted this future sister to be named Jasmine. So this wedding day was going to be so special! I had no idea that the wedding ceremony was in jeopardy and might not take place.

Geoffrey and I lived in a house that I was renting from my brother Larry not far from where Mom and Dad lived. After helping Geoffrey get dressed, we left the house. I was elated and so excited! God had truly blessed me. With so many hopes for a bright future, Geoffrey and I were going to start a new life.

As I drove along the road en route to my parents' house, I noticed that the traffic in my lane was no longer moving. I brought the car to a complete stop and proceeded to wait for the cars in front of us to move again. As we sat there, I happened to look up into my rear-view mirror and saw a car barreling toward us. Apparently, the driver did not realize that traffic had stopped. I threw my right arm across Geoffrey's chest, like my mom had done when I was a child, to protect him from the impending impact. It happened so fast that I didn't even have time to pray. The driver had no recourse but to slam into the back of my car. As I braced for the impending impact, nothing happened. The next thing I knew his car was over to my right, on the shoulder of the road.

I couldn't believe that he didn't hit our car. His vehicle came too close and should have slammed into us. It was as if something or someone moved his car to the shoulder without even scraping my car. I sat there, literally shaking, realizing that I had just witnessed a miracle. I knew that the driver was shaken because he did not even get out of the car and was probably trying to figure out why he did not plow into us. All I know is that the driver did not even skid or lose control. I had been the victim of previous car accidents, and I knew that at the speed at which he was traveling, he should have hit me or at the very least, lost control of his vehicle. I thanked God for protecting us and will always believe that an angel moved his car. I was shaken yet filled with joy and gratitude, so grateful that this special day was not destroyed by a tragedy. I knew that God had indeed blessed us with His protection.

After the car incident, we continued on our way. I got to the house and changed into my wedding clothes. The ceremony was beautiful with family and close friends there to celebrate with us. It proved to be one of the happiest days of my life. Life was going to be so much better than ever before. I had no idea of the life-changing challenges that loomed ahead.

Wedding Day
Arie, Charles and Geoffrey

Wedding Day with Family

**Wedding Day with Darryl,
Marilyn and Andrea**

Chapter 2

LABOR OF LOVE

"Twins," I said. "No, I can't be pregnant with twins," I thought as I lay on the examination table in my gynecologist's office. My Ob-Gyn (obstetrics and gynecology) doctor and his nurse were so happy and excited. However, I became numb with the reality that they were not joking, and I really was pregnant with *twins*! Charles and I technically were still newlyweds, and I had gone just to get an Ob-Gyn checkup. I couldn't believe it.

Lying there on the table and oblivious to everything, the words of the diagnosis began to penetrate my mind. My doctor spoke, and his voice jarred me. "Mrs. Gray, there are impending precautions with this type of pregnancy, especially because of your age," he said. With a concerned tone in his voice, he said, "The main precaution is that you will need to stop working. At some point, that may be during or near the end of your fifth month of pregnancy. At that point, I will have to take you out of work." I thought to myself, "No he's not...that's crazy," and I mumbled, "I will work as long as I can." He replied, "Trust me, you will be very glad for me to make you stop working." I couldn't believe all of this. "Lord," I asked, "how can this be happening to me?"

After Charles and I walked around in shock for several days, we knew that we would have to obey the doctor's advice. Our faith was strong, and we were trusting in God to see us through.

At first, I started enjoying pregnancy again. I ordered some cute maternity clothes and received some really nice outfits from my cousin Danita. Geoffrey was quite excited that I was

5

going to have twins. One day, as he and I were riding home from the store, I asked him, "What do you think the babies are, two boys, two girls, or one of each?" He was very quiet. I asked him again, "Geoffrey, did you hear me? What do you think the babies are?" He then shocked me by saying, "God just told me in my mind that they are both girls." A short time later, I had a sonogram, which showed that the babies appeared to be girls.

Believing in God every step of the way, our trust in Him was soon tested. First, I started having problems with my left breast. A medical test determined that I would need a biopsy. I was given local anesthesia and soon it was discovered that part of a milk gland needed to be removed. My doctor conducted the procedure, and although I was offered stronger pain medication, I refused it, as I did not want to do anything that might endanger the health of the babies. As the anesthesia wore off, I realized that this would not be easy. It felt as if metal nails were stabbing my breast. I used ice and acetaminophen for the pain, which did not help. I even went to work the next day and participated on a hiring panel. Periodically, I tried not to wince as the metal nails continued to remind me of the previous day's procedure. Fortunately, there was no evidence of malignancy from the biopsy, and I was grateful. Little did I know that this brief "hiccup" would not compare to the dilemma that lay ahead.

During my fourth month of pregnancy, I went into pre-term labor. That morning, I thought I was experiencing indigestion, but something told me to call my doctor. He told me to come to his office so that he could check my status. Once we got there, he determined that I was having contractions and told Charles to immediately take me to the hospital. My contractions began to dissipate, much to the relief of everyone. It was too soon for the girls to be born. I was admitted into the hospital and monitored closely for several days.

Staring at the hospital walls and listening to the solitude of my spirit, I prayed often. I knew in my heart that God heard my prayers, that he was going to save my babies and make everything alright. God had never failed me, and I knew His love would not disappoint me. Sure enough, my condition became fully stabilized, and I was released from the hospital. "Thank you, Lord," I said, "for allowing us to get through this crisis."

But things did not return to normal. "You cannot return to work," my doctor stated. "I am prescribing complete bed rest and an oral medication to prevent any more pre-term labor. You can either be on bedrest in the hospital or bedrest at home." Of course, I chose to go home. Lord, have mercy! I couldn't believe this was happening to me. Once home in bed, which now felt like a prison cell, I looked at a calendar. Estimating how many months I would spend in bed, I felt the tears well up in my eyes. I could not exist like a normal person, not even to walk around the house. No more driving a car, shopping, or even walking to the bathroom. "Okay God," I said, "Please, please help me get through this."

Confined to the use of a wheelchair, the doctor permitted me to go from one room to another but only a few times a week. As I lay in the bed, I watched as Charles placed a potty chair by my side of the bed. My health insurance covered a home health care aide, who helped take care of me some of the time, along with a nurse who took my vitals several times a week. Charles waited on me constantly, supplying me with whatever I needed or wanted. He also put a small refrigerator and microwave by the bed. To help lift my spirits, he would sometimes set up the electric keyboard on the bed so we could play and sing gospel songs.

Since Charles had to work Monday through Friday, Mom was my primary company and took great care of me. This allowed us to spend a lot of quality time together. Dad also helped by taking care of their household matters, as Mom spent most of her time with me. Mom's sister, Aunt Woncey, sent me a box of goodies each month. Every day, I anxiously waited to open one of the goodies, which were small and delicately wrapped gifts.

The amount of responsibility was enormous, and Charles had a lot to deal with. Now that I was going to be out of work for a significant amount of time, we didn't know what kind of financial impact this would have on our family. Fortunately, there was a program that allowed employers to give leave to "hardship" cases, such as mine. Members of our home church, i.e. Sargent Memorial, also donated leave and encouraged associates to do so. This proved to be such a blessing to us, and because of the generosity of so many, I continued to receive my salary until January 3, 1995. Another challenge was that Charles needed help with groceries and daily food preparation. Late one night (he told me later), he went to the kitchen, feeling somewhat overwhelmed by everything that was going on. He prayed to the Lord for help and of course, the Lord heard his prayer. He received a phone call the next day from his home church, First Baptist Church of Merrifield, stating that they would start bringing us food each week, which would be more than enough to last throughout the week. God truly blessed us and supplied all of our needs. I had a great team—a wonderful husband, parents, family, churches, choir members, and friends. It was indeed a labor of love!

Despite my doctor's efforts, there were more complications. I had begun having significant acid reflux and had to sleep propped up with pillows. Then more complications occurred. There were pulled groin muscles that resulted from me (yes, I cheated) walking twice to the living room to help celebrate my brother's birthday, instead of using the wheelchair. Being confined to bed rest had caused my muscles to weaken. Also, the babies' weight increased the severity of the muscle pull. Now I understood when football players say they cannot play because of strained groin muscles that they are not being "wimps." The pain was very real, and every time I moved my body just a little, the muscles hurt.

The worst complication came in the form of fibroid tumors. As time progressed, the fibroid tumors grew and became more painful. Soon, the pain from the tumors felt like someone was stabbing my abdomen with a hot poker and holding it there for several minutes at a time. There was never-ending pain and discomfort. As the babies grew, the pain intensified. I did not take strong pain medication because that could jeopardize the babies' welfare. Sometimes at night, I would lie there and cry silently so as not to wake up Charles. I prayed and prayed, "God please take this pain away." Through the tears, though, I remembered how Jesus suffered on the cross. I could only imagine the pain He suffered for us. I knew that somehow I had to survive.

By August 30, 1994 the pain from the growing fibroids was so severe that I would put my pillow in my mouth to keep from screaming. I knew I could not survive this level of unbearable pain anymore. Charles called our doctor, and we headed to the hospital. It was time for Jasmine and Jessica, though premature, to make their entrance into the world. Charles was with me in the delivery room the entire time, and I was so happy that this was almost over. My doctor had given me an epidural, which numbs the lower body, so much of the pain was gone. I was so relieved that my suffering was almost over. Despite being in labor, I even began cracking jokes. Among chuckles resulting from my silly jokes, my doctor administered an episiotomy, which would help eliminate the pain of labor and the probability of my skin tearing during the delivery.

Soon, Jasmine came out. However, Jessica was breech and unfortunately, would not come out. Suddenly, my blood pressure escalated to a dangerous level. I could see the monitor and saw that the bottom number, the diastolic, had reached 124. I sensed the immediate concern of the medical team, resulting in my doctor giving me an injection, which immediately put me to sleep. He then delivered Jessica by emergency Cesarean. When I awoke in the recovery room, I found out that my daughters each weighed a little more than four pounds. Jasmine and Jessica remained in the neonatal intensive care unit but were going to be fine. Yes, I had delivered them both ways, vaginal and c-section. We were all ecstatic and thanked God for blessing us with these two little girls.

As I had lost a lot of blood during the delivery, they almost administered a blood transfusion. Since I could have suffered a stroke and my blood pressure was still quite elevated, I stayed longer in the hospital than normal. I was released on the Saturday before Labor Day and was finally at home! Unfortunately, I still had to rest in bed, wear compression stockings to prevent circulatory problems, and use a wheelchair. Having been bedridden for so long, my muscles had lost their strength so I would need time to heal and become stronger. On that Sunday, I was told that Mom was in her "glory" at our home church, Sargent Memorial Presbyterian Church. She told everyone about the babies, and everyone was thrilled!

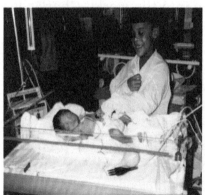

**Geoffrey and the Babies
in NICU**

**Mom Bertha and Arie
Holding the Babies**

It was September 7, 1994, the Tuesday after that Labor Day weekend. The babies were still in the hospital, Charles was at work, and Geoffrey was at school. The worst was over. I still could not walk without assistance and of course, needed the wheelchair. My blood pressure was elevated. Mom had just gotten me settled in the bed. After she left the bedroom to get me some lunch, my dad yelled frantically from the living room for me to call 911. Evidently, Mom was having some type of attack. I grabbed the phone, immediately called 911, and limped out to the living room. Mom was lying on the sofa, saying over and over again, "Oh Jesus, I don't know what's wrong with me." Coach Wells, one of our neighbors and Charles' high school track instructor, was outside in our yard trimming some bushes. We yelled for him; he rushed in and tried to assist us. The rescue squad came, checked Mom's vitals, attached an IV, and rushed her to the nearest hospital.

That hour in the ER waiting room, we waited, prayed, and tried not to worry. We sang gospel songs and knew that God would get us through another dilemma. Sitting in the wheelchair, Charles pushed me out into the lobby to a pay telephone. I called loved ones, co-workers, friends, and anyone else whose number I could remember, asking them to pray for Mom. My cousin Rose came to the hospital to be with us. While they worked on Mom, the emergency room staff would not let us see her. We had paged my brother Larry (my only sibling), a physician himself. He was attending a medical symposium, at least an hour away from the hospital. Hopefully, he would get to us soon.

We continued to pray and felt that this could not be a matter of life-and-death. This was a mild attack, nothing serious, I reasoned. Soon the doctors came and gave us the news, just as Larry rushed into the waiting room: "We are so sorry... we did everything we could to save her." I heard crying and realized that it was Denise, one of my choir members, who was part of the team that had worked on Mom. She was a respiratory therapist and while working in the ER that day, Mom was the first patient in the ER whom she personally knew. She was overcome with grief, as she had known my mother for many years. A short time later, she told us that she had held Mom's hand and heard her final words, asking if someone could give her something because she was so tired. Although I was grateful that Denise had been there with Mom, the new reality was still the same. Mom was gone, one week after the birth of Jasmine and Jessica. Gone! Larry requested an autopsy be done and days later, it was determined that Mom had died of a pulmonary embolism. How could this happen? How?

I wanted to die. I simply wanted to die. I felt this was a terrible nightmare and that I would wake up. But I was awake, and this was not a dream. My mother, best friend, and big sister, all rolled up into one person, was gone. How could I go on? "God, how could you let this happen to us? How could you let this happen to me?" I asked. We were all in shock! I guessed that mom had died from a heart attack and maybe the stress of my pregnancy had caused her death. As Charles, Rose and I rode back to our house, I stopped crying long enough to say, "I killed my mother." Rose immediately told me to stop saying this and lovingly reminded me that this was not true—*and* that I was not God. "You do not have the power to decide life and death," she said. I buried my face into my hands.

Devastation is a mild term for what we felt that September. The agony, for Larry and me, was monumental. Again, how could God allow this to happen? Charles begged me to fight to survive this: "Arie, please don't die. Please live for me, Geoffrey, Jasmine, and Jessica. Please live; we love you; I love you."

I was sedated during the weekend of mom's funeral. Today, I still do not remember most of the people who attended the funeral. Two days after she was buried, Jasmine and Jessica came home from the hospital. The labor of love continued, as we faced the challenge of taking care of two tiny premature babies. Initially we had to feed them every two hours. Gradually, I became physically stronger. However, my faith in God was shattered. I blamed God for this. Someone had to be blamed for Mom's sudden death. Then I decided that if God wasn't to blame, then my complicated pregnancy was responsible for this tragedy. Despite what Rose had said, I still believed I had caused Mom's death. The pain from this guilt was unbearable.

Late one night, a few weeks after Mom's death, I was lying in bed trying to go to sleep. Suddenly, I began to have severe pains on the left side of my chest. Charles immediately called 911. Once emergency medical technicians arrived, they took my vitals and determined that although my blood pressure was elevated, I was not having a heart attack. However, they stated that Charles could still take me to the hospital, which was only five minutes away or they could still take me. Charles stated he would take me himself. Dad was there staying with us temporarily, so leaving the children at home would be fine.

Unfortunately, this was the same emergency room where Mom had died. Charles had called Larry to let him know what was going on and soon, he got to the emergency room. I will never forget watching him from across the room, conversing with the doctor in charge. Tests were run on me, and it was determined that my chest pains were not because of a heart attack. However, the doctor told me that I needed to follow up with my regular doctor, which I did. Months later, I was diagnosed by a cardiologist with Mitral Valve Prolapse. This condition had caused the chest pains, and the blood pressure medication I began taking soon after the birth of the girls was adjusted to curtail chest pain occurrences.

Although we were grateful that I did not have a heart attack, this experience was quite traumatic, especially since I had now revisited the very place where Mom had died. It was as if someone had, as the expression says, "poured salt into a wound." Not only that but my mind was reliving Mom's sudden death and the anguish that still continued.

One evening while Charles was out running errands, I found myself standing in front of the bathroom medicine cabinet. I opened it and quickly found enough pills that if taken, would end my life. The children were asleep, and the house was quiet. I thought, "I can do this." I could not continue to live with this amount of pain and grief. It had to stop. This was going to be my way out. I stood there staring at those pills for what seemed to be an eternity. But the Spirit of God kept me from making the biggest mistake of my life. I slumped to the floor and cried. I realized that somehow, despite how I felt, I had to live. Years later, I realized that I likely had postpartum depression, which was disguised by the grief of Mom's death. I really should have had counseling and two years later, when I felt as if I had run into a brick wall, I did engage in counseling. To this very day, I recommend it, preferably spiritual counseling, which is not a sign of weakness, but a sign of strength!

Finally, I resumed some of my normal activities. Thank God, I could drive the car, go shopping, and do other things I had been unable to do during the pregnancy. Though I was still upset with God for allowing the pain, suffering, and Mom's death to occur, the Lord ministered to me through conversations initiated by strangers. The first group of people had lost loved ones who died from pulmonary embolisms. This was so strange. These were total strangers in store waiting lines or other venues, striking up conversations with me, and discussing what happened to them and their loved ones.

The next small group of strangers were those who, as children, had lost their mothers. One lady stopped me outside a CVS drug store. She was selling makeup for the Mary Kay cosmetics company. I kindly told her that I was not interested in purchasing makeup and that I was just trying to survive. She asked me if I was okay, and I then told her about losing Mom. To my surprise, she informed me that her mother had died when she was a little girl and began to share what had happened in her life. This wonderful lady encouraged me with kind words and before she departed, gave me a hug.

A few days later, I stopped by a local mall and went into a pizza shop for lunch. I purchased a slice of pizza, sat at one of the tables near the windows, and tried to eat. Tears quietly flowed down my face. Suddenly, the young man who had served me the pizza was standing in front of me. He asked, "May I sit down," and of course, I replied, "Yes." Now, this Italian, nice-looking young man was asking me, "Miss, are you okay?" I quickly told him that my mom had recently died and that she and I had eaten together in this pizzeria a few years ago. Again, a conversational surprise: He told me that his mother had died when he was five years old. This kind young man talked a little about life without his mother and told me that I would make it. I thanked him for talking to me.

Shortly before Christmas, I went to a nearby mall to look for a few Christmas gifts. The mall was beautifully decorated with lights and the sounds of Christmas carols filled the air. This was our first Christmas without Mom, and I was feeling very depressed. I spotted a newly opened children's store and went in to look at clothes for Jasmine and Jessica. Apparently, the employees of this new store had been instructed to greet customers with "Good morning and how are you today?" This happened to me a couple of times, causing my mood to worsen. Their greeting, frankly, was getting on my nerves. Finally, a young employee who appeared to be in her mid-twenties repeated the mantra, "Good morning and how are you today?" I looked at her and responded curtly, "Well if you really want to know, I am not having such a good day today. My mother died a couple of months ago. This is my first Christmas without her, but *you* wouldn't understand that now, would you?!" She stared at me for a moment; then her facial expression saddened. As tears began to fall from her eyes, she then told me that her mother died when she was 17 years old.

Amazing how God works, isn't it? Now, here I was consoling this young woman. She talked about how she felt her life would have been more productive if her mother were alive to encourage her. I felt terrible about how I had initially spoken to her but now said what I could to make her feel better.

After I left the store, I stopped at a nearby bookstore in the mall to purchase a book I had started reading. It was entitled *Motherless Daughters*. It contained letters from women who had lost their mothers at various stages in their lives. The young employee from the children's store was surprised when I returned to the store later that week, carrying a gift wrapped in red Christmas paper. When I handed it to her, she thanked me, and we hugged one another. She did not realize that her gift to me was the story of her loss and how the death of her mother had impacted her life. This young woman was a gentle reminder that I was blessed to have had a loving mother for 39 years, instead of 17 years. When I left the store, I spoke out loud to the Lord, and said "Okay, God. I get it. You placed three strangers in my path to remind me that some have lost mothers during their childhood. I get it." Weeks later, I returned to the children's store to look for the young woman. She wasn't there, and I never saw her again.

There were many other instances when the Lord used people, total strangers, to share their experiences with me. I realized that these conversations were more than coincidental. These strangers were a comfort and a reminder that I was blessed. As time passed by, my faith in the Lord began to grow again. I begged God to forgive me for being angry with Him and to give me strength to continue my life. God answered my prayer and continued to bless me each day.

One day, something happened that I will always remember. The girls were both sitting in their little baby carriers on our bed. I don't remember what I was doing, but I stopped because I noticed something incredible. Both Jasmine and Jessica were staring at the farthest corner of our bedroom, gazing at the ceiling. Not only were they staring, but they were wearing huge grins, as if what they were looking at was the most beautiful thing they had ever seen. They were transfixed! I immediately believed that something or someone was in the room with us. Was it an angel? Was it Mom? All I know is that I started talking aloud to whomever it was, as if it were my mother and I felt a sense of peace. As my tears fell, I thanked God that maybe, just maybe, he had allowed Mom to visit us for a moment. I will never forget that moment, and it never happened again.

A few years after the birth of the babies, I was sitting in the kitchen humming a gospel song that deals with God "preparing me for something that I can't handle right now." It was a quiet moment. Suddenly, a wave of understanding came over me. I had always questioned God about why He allowed me to suffer such physical pain during my pregnancy. His gentle voice in my mind told me, in that quiet moment sitting in the kitchen, that He had allowed the pain and suffering in order to build me up and to prepare me for the enormity of Mom's death. That suffering had made me stronger. In that calm instant, I finally understood. I began to cry but found myself smiling through my tears. I finally realized that although I may not have understood everything that occurred in my life, God loved me. In that moment, I bowed my head and thanked Him for Mom, His forgiveness, and most of all, His love.

Yes, the labor of love I experienced was special. It contained joy, sorrow, happiness, heartache, extreme pain, and at times doubts and concerns for the future. Mom's labor of love began in her womb where she carried me. She loved me my entire life and unselfishly sacrificed the last few months of her life for her granddaughters and me. Yet, God's labor of love was the greatest sacrifice of all, His Son, Jesus Christ. He blessed me by keeping me alive, as I could have suffered a fatal stroke. He blessed me by comforting and helping me, even using strangers along the way to convey His love. In the years that followed, He continued to show me even more of His blessings from above.

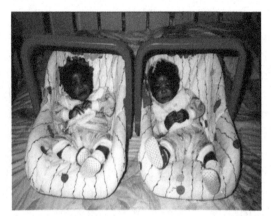

Jasmine and Jessica In Their Carriers

* * * * *

And now, Charles will share
some of his memories in the next chapter.

Chapter 3

CHARLES REMEMBERS

Even though I (Charles) always put the thought out of my mind, I always knew that someday I would allow myself to be drawn into the life of serving the Lord. After all, answering the call would result in giving myself totally to Him. I am eternally thankful, however, that the Lord thought more of me than I thought of myself. So how did this truly blessed life of ministry with an amazing woman and family all happen?

From the time I can remember, I would imitate my father. He was a real preacher, and yes, he "brought the fire" when he preached. I remember that as a child, I would go behind the house with my "congregation," which consisted of my two dogs and one cat. I would get a couple of cinderblocks and stand them on their sides. (I had to have a pulpit you know.) There I would preach to my dogs and cat, imitating Dad as best I could. I recall my dad saying that if I had stayed on that path, he would have had me preaching to people. Anyway, the dogs and cats seemed to listen and that is as far as it went for the next 35 years. I wandered about as far away from God as a person could go and still be alive. The funny thing about God is that He does not give up on you. Through all my running away from Him, He just kept on pursuing me. Despite all my faults and weaknesses, God just kept coming. As the late Andre Crouch, legendary Gospel artist penned, "...to God be the glory for the things He has done." I can attest not only that God has kept me alive, but that God has done many miraculous things for me.

On August 20, 1983, my dad got sick for the last time. I remember I went to see him, a visit I will never forget. At that time of my life, I was far removed from going anywhere near a church. My life had pretty much spiraled out of control, and I had become a "wretch" indeed. Yet I still sensed somehow that God was there. On that hot August day, I went to visit my dad in the hospital. He had been very sick. To my surprise, I found him sitting up in the bed, looking like he was going home one more time. Although I was intoxicated, wearing my dark sunglasses, shamefully and reluctantly, I found myself standing at the foot of his bed. I am so glad I was there, as it would be the last time I would see my father alive and boy, did he lay a "whopper" on me. He was so full of strength and presence that it appeared that the Lord was not done with him. Yet, looking back, God did have at least one more assignment for Dad. That was me. I tried to talk about him getting out of the hospital and going home, but Dad was not interested in hearing any of that. He kept changing the conversation back to me. Soon I became tired, more like uncomfortable, with Dad's continued advice and guidance. I made some excuse to leave, telling him I would see him soon, and that was when he changed my life forever. I suppose the Lord must have given Dad a sense that I had not received his words to me, and he reached for my hand. He looked at me, told me to take off the sunglasses, and then simply said to me, "Son, fix your eyes."

Now I was fully ashamed of myself for going to see my sick father in my impaired state. It took years before I understood what he really meant by those last words to me. I was ashamed of myself for many years, thinking I had disappointed my father, that I had failed miserably at making him proud of me. For years, I kept doing even worse things to myself and others. I was lost, but God just kept on coming. When my dad passed away, I would never forget his last words to me. He wanted me to realize that my eyes, my focus, was selfishly on myself, on the world, and not the Lord. I am so glad that God gave him those words that I will never forget.

I stumbled through the next 15 years or so, ashamed of myself but never letting anyone know. I just covered it up with some façade or pretense. Over the years I had become rather successful at my job but on the inside, and at home, I was a "hot mess." I had become angry at the Lord, angry at the world, and I still harbored the feeling that I had disappointed my father. Yes indeed, I even made God the problem. How could He allow my faithful father to be reduced to having to be physically carried into the pulpit and allow him to suffer so much? Yep, God was a good target, and for years, He stayed my main target.

I am so glad, however, that God just kept on coming, pursuing me. Over the course of those years, He sent many people to me—some I knew, most I did not know. The one thing they all had in common was they would somehow remind me that God had a calling on my life, and that I would someday become a preacher. Boy, I was having none of that talk. I remember saying some awful things to those kind people, who I now know were God's messengers to me, and if I could now, I would ask each of them to forgive me.

One day, I was about to have lunch, and I wanted to be alone. So, I went to a little basement eatery down the street from my building. This lunch time changed my life and my dad's words would finally ring true to me. While I was successful in getting away from everybody on the job that day, God knew exactly where I was. I did not know it, but God was about to heal my broken soul. I was successful in finding a place to eat alone, at least I thought I had. The little eatery was empty, and there was nobody to bother me. Great!

After getting my food, I selected a little table, sat down, and began to eat. A gentleman appeared at my table and asked if he could join me. I thought to myself, "What?" but I said, "Sure." The gentlemen looked to be about ready to retire so I did not want to be rude. He sat down across from me and began to tell me about himself, though I must admit I can't recall where he worked or even his name. What I can say is that I remember he seemed to be very kind, and soon I found myself talking, I mean really talking, telling him things I seldomly expressed to anyone, let alone a total stranger. He asked me about work and family and for some reason I admitted that while on the outside I appeared to have it "all together," on the inside I was a mess. I even told him how I had disappointed my dad not only in life but even the very last time I saw him alive. By this time my eyes were swelling with tears. I was feeling the familiar rush of guilt and shame coming over me, and here I was, telling my story to a man I did not even know.

He listened to me without saying a word and when I finished, he said these words to me, "I know your dad is proud of you. Look at what you have become." While I was all caught up in my moment of grief and shame, I had missed the present tense he spoke in. He encouraged me to forgive myself, and said that if I were his son, he would not be disappointed but proud of how I had not given up. "Just look at what you have become," he stated. The kind man finished his lunch and said something to the effect that he enjoyed our time together and hoped to see me in the future. I remember he mentioned that he worked somewhere in the building, and I desperately wanted to see him again. I went back to the basement eatery many times, but I never saw the gentleman again.

After he left, I stayed at the table for a while trying to compose myself and returned to work with the kind man's words ringing in my head, "I know your dad is proud of you." As the Apostle Paul wrote in 2 Corinthians 12:2, "Whether this man [is] in the body, I cannot tell; or whether out of the body, I cannot tell: God knoweth." What I do know today for sure is that God reached out to me and began to heal my broken soul that very day. All I can say is, "Thank you, Lord." I didn't deserve anything. After all, God was my biggest target of anger, yet He just kept on pursuing me; He kept coming.

I soon found myself sitting on the back bench of my home church, still broken, but back home at last. I stayed in the back row every Sunday, listening to the sermons and the singing for quite a while. They had two services, and the early service was my preference. I remember running out the door as soon as Pastor finished the benediction (a blessing at the end of a worship service), yet I knew I was being convicted to draw closer to God. Looking back, I suppose I could have hurt someone, accidentally knocking them down, getting out of the church in such a hurry. Despite my stubbornness, God kept pursuing me. It was not long before He touched me, and I started to grow. I soon found my way back into music ministry, which I had abandoned, and was now playing the organ and piano again. Yes, I was back home and growing. However, I was still running out of the church as soon as Pastor said, "Amen!" Picture this, there are two exit doors at the front of the sanctuary; one is located behind the organ, the other behind the piano. So as soon as the benediction ended, I was out of one of those two doors. Silly right? It took a couple of years, but God changed my life and my attitudes. Now, He was all that mattered. I was now studying the Bible, conducting choir rehearsals, and playing keyboards for back-to-back services. I hardly noticed that I had become one of those "church people."

There was a major music department change on the horizon and I did not welcome it. Frankly, however, it changed my life and then "she" marched right in. One of the choirs I played for decided, due to the music department's reorganization, to have one last anniversary celebration, preceding the dissolvement of the group forever. So, we prepared for our final concert together. We had invited a well-known choir out of Washington, D.C., the Sargent Gospel-Aires, to be our guest choir.

I will never forget that day. I actually wrote a musical piece for our choir to march in on. (In case you didn't know, gospel choirs like to march.) Anyway, the pianist that accompanied me was unable to learn the song by the day of the concert and had positioned herself in a chair well away from the piano itself. The program started and so I began to play for the first time ever in public, "We Come to Praise Him." I was at the organ, doing all I could to make it sound full. The choir and church were thoroughly into the music. The mood was festive and then I heard the piano playing along with the song. Yes, there were beautiful sounds coming from the piano, so I thought my pianist had decided to give it a try. I craned my neck around our big Allen organ to give a thumbs up to the pianist and that was when I saw "her." This young woman was sitting there playing my song, just as if she had practiced with me. Boy was I impressed! God was in full swing now. As fate would have it, she and I, by the end of the program, were sitting on the first pew, right beside each other. I don't remember much more of the concert, God forgive me, but I could not stop looking and gazing at the woman who had played my song.

Anyway, at the end of our church services, our pastor would sometimes do a little benediction that included taking the hands of your "neighbor" (the person sitting next to you), looking into their eyes, and repeating whatever the pastor said. Truthfully, all I can remember in the case of this "neighbor," was that somehow, I knew I had found her, the woman I would marry. This amazing woman who played my song, has been playing it ever since. Now isn't God good? Not only had He kept pursuing me, but now He delivered me right to the love of my life. Yes, God has done great things for me, truly great things. After a year or so of dating, I asked Arie to marry me. She said yes, and do you believe it, she was so perfect for me. She was a Christian; she was smart; she was attractive; and me, I could still use a lot of work, right? Anyway, we got married and soon we found out that she was having twins!

After a very complicated pregnancy, the babies were born. In a few short years I went from hardly caring about anything to now having a wife, a stepson, and twins. Oh my gosh!

Due to the restructuring of the music department at my home church and meeting Arie, I became a musician in the choir she co-directed, the Sargent Gospel-Aires. Since the choir sang one Sunday per month, we started visiting other churches in the area, including both our home churches. I realize now that God wanted to show me some things in the body of Christ and to also get my attention. He accomplished both. It is kind of funny in retrospect, but I never really knew where we were going on any particular Sunday. We would just get in the car, and Arie would ask, "Where are we going today?" I would answer, "I'm not sure," and then we would end up at a church.

By this time the Lord was well at work in me, calling me to preach the Gospel of Jesus Christ. I fought it for a good while, but one Sunday we were returning from a concert, and I just looked at my wife and said, "The Lord is calling me to preach." After much prayer and hesitation, I began to prepare myself to become a minister. I even resigned from my job so that I could devote myself to full-time study. That decision was life changing. Arie and I prayed a lot for wisdom, and the Lord financially made a way. While I had several mentors, Dr. T. W. Morris (Aunt Woncey's husband, who by that time had pastored churches for almost fifty years) was the main blessing who guided me and encouraged me throughout my time of preparation and ordination into ministry. I remember my graduation day from Trinity College and Seminary. The graduation ceremony was in Evansville, Indiana. My wife and children, my mom, my sister Joyce, my brother-in-law Larry, and Arie's father all traveled a long distance to celebrate with me receiving my divinity degree. As you might imagine, I was very touched that anyone would do this for me, and I am forever grateful.

However, with all the wonderful surprises that occurred on that special graduation day, one was so unexpected. We were all sitting at the graduation dinner and in walk Dr. T.W. Morris and Eleanor Morris, aka Aunt Woncey. They had driven all that way from Virginia to Indiana for me, and I was so deeply moved. Even today, those memories cause me to become emotional. Dr. Morris, aka Uncle T, would often check on me and keep me motivated. He seemed to always know when to call me, most times unexpectedly, and would simply say, "And how is Charles doing today?" He and my mother have now gone to be with the Lord. I miss you Mom, I miss you Uncle T, and I thank you both.

Well, back to not knowing which church it would be on any particular Sunday. On this Sunday, Arie again asked, "Where are we going today?" and I replied, "I am not sure." We ended up this Sunday at a church where the Lord would again communicate very clearly to me that I had been called to preach God's gospel. This church, which I had passed by so many times, was now where I parked our car. As we entered the church, I remember the folks at the door being nice enough, but they immediately wanted to take our babies and whisk them off to their nursery. Arie was not about to give up her babies to anybody. After all, she almost died having them so no, no one was taking the babies anywhere. So funny again in retrospect. If the church people had insisted that the babies go to their nursery, we would have left the church and I would have missed what God was about to do directly for me.

I did not realize it at the time, but this church was a "59-minute" church, which means that the service is literally an hour in length, including the benediction. Wow, how did I end up here? My home church services were often two hours in length. This was also a very quiet church. I remember that Jasmine started to whimper a bit and even though Arie did all she could to quiet her, the whimper came out. It was if we had broken a glass window or something, as most of the congregation briefly turned around in their seats toward us. They looked as if they were mentally saying, *"There is a baby in here!"* Oh boy, should we leave? Well, we remained in the service, slightly offended, but now, we were "dug in" for the long haul.

Again, God was about to do great things for me, and I am very thankful that we stayed for the entire service. Everything was crisp and straight forward. A scripture, a prayer, a hymn with all the verses, and then the offering. However, I still was unaware they were on a 59-minute time schedule. After all was done, the preacher, an elderly white gentleman, rose to give the sermon. I thought to myself, "What is going on here?" Here we are in an African American Baptist church, and they have an elderly white pastor. As the expression goes, "Not what I was expecting."

I cannot as of this writing tell you what the preacher's text was or his sermon topic. I was still marveling that he was the pastor. A short way into his message, he stopped, looked out over the congregation, and said these words that I will never forget. "Someone here today needs to know that God wants one more preacher." He went on to say, "I have been preaching for 50 years, and I have been in a lot of churches and pulpits. Over the course of this time, God has shown me that if ten percent of them were preaching and teaching the Word of God, that that would be a generous summation of what I have seen." He proceeded to reiterate again that, "Someone here today needs to know that God wants one more preacher." Now, not only does he have my attention, but tears are now streaming down my face. God had found me again! I had not known where I was going that morning, no idea really, but God knew. My very argument laid bare before me—all the preachers and all the churches, seemingly on every corner. I knew that God was calling me to preach but I still questioned it. I wanted confirmation. God had answered my question directly, and I was overcome with emotion. Knowing better now how God works, there may have been other hesitant preachers in the service that day. However, I was there for sure, and for little ole me, God heard my heart cry, "So many churches, so many preachers, why would you possibly want another preacher?"

Then the preacher returned to his message, leading to an important announcement. At the end of his message, he announced that he would be retiring as their pastor. He explained that he had spent his entire adult life preaching the Word of God and pastoring. Boy, that changed everything, and the time was 11:59 a.m. He gave the benediction and the congregation said, "Amen!"

I really wanted to meet the pastor at this point, to shake his hand, and tell him that God had used him to speak directly to me; but after his retirement announcement, there was no getting anywhere near him. Everyone was standing in a rather long line to talk to him about his bombshell retirement announcement. With two hungry babies, and one not feeling so well (Jasmine, the one who whimpered), we decided that we would come back and visit very soon. Perhaps then I could shake the pastor's hand.

It was only two weeks before we would go back to that church. I really wanted to shake the pastor's hand and speak with him, but it was not meant to be. As we arrived in the sanctuary, I detected a feeling of sadness. I could not tell why, but it did not take long to find out that this gentle man of God, this preacher I will never forget, had been dead and buried for nearly two weeks. I was in a state of shock and amazement, which remains even to this day. You see, God had spoken to me with an audible voice on that earlier Sunday morning. He used a man who seemed odd to me at first, at a church I probably would never have gone back to, as it was so different from the "spirited" services I was used to attending. Yet, that was where God met me and straightened me out. Believe it or not, the Lord still was not finished! We visited another Baptist church nearby and this preacher virtually said exactly what the previous pastor (now deceased) had articulated. God was again telling me to preach. The main difference was that this minister was not retiring. However, a week or so later, we heard that this minister had also died. As the Apostle Paul wrote in 1 Corinthians 9:16, "Woe unto me if I preach not the gospel."

I have done my best since that time to do just that, to preach the gospel to anybody who has the ears to hear it. With over 28 years of marriage to an amazing woman, I know I have been blessed by God. He has given me a God-fearing wife, a life-tested true best friend, and a more-than-willing and able partner who has embraced God's calling on our lives. I have witnessed His hand on her life, for while she has as many struggles as we all do, she engages them with a grace that only God can provide.

I remember on one of our first dates, while sitting in her parents' living room, I opened their large family Bible to Genesis 2:18 and said to Arie, "I want to ask you a question." She replied, "Okay, what's your question?" I read Genesis 2:18 to her, which states this: "And the Lord God said, it is not good that the man should be alone; I will make him an help meet for him." I asked her, can you do this? She paused for a few seconds. I understood her pausing, as I am sure this is not how most people converse during early dating. She said "I'm assuming that a help meet is a helper or companion. Correct?" "That's right, I replied." My dear Arie, after a few moments, answered with a resounding, "Yes I can." I want you all to know, that yes, she has!

I remember that God blessed me by using total strangers and ministers of the gospel to communicate with me. My prayer is that He will continue to use my wife and me to bring Him glory, honor and praise!!

* * * * *

And now, let me turn the "pulpit" back to
Arie in the next chapter.

Chapter 4

SPIRITUAL HEALING

When Jasmine and Jessica were toddlers, it was apparent to Charles and I that they needed help. We didn't have a diagnosis yet, but we knew they needed healing. They were very delayed in virtually every aspect of their development. In faith, I printed out pages of healing scriptures and taped them around the perimeter of their little bedroom. I prayed and trusted in God. I knew that He would heal them.

But it hurt deep inside me to see them struggle. They were so cute, and when we went out to events, people would often gravitate to us. Remember, they were identical twins, and unfortunately, the people attracted to our children experienced only their babbling or silence. In contrast, Geoffrey at three years old, had been such a talker. When I would prepare to read him a bedtime story, he could even verbally identify the book's title page. Jasmine and Jessica's little lives were so different. For instance, taking them to another child's birthday party usually included awkward moments. As my girls would be playing, you could visually see that the other little children around their age would quickly realize that they really couldn't talk. A parent sitting next to me would ask, "How old are your daughters?" Once I told them, a pregnant pause would occur. I knew what this parent was thinking, "Then why aren't they talking?" I would usually volunteer a quick explanation, which was that the girls were preemies, that they had some delays, but that God had brought us through. These are some of the many experiences parents like us have gone through.

My friend Beverly from my workplace headed a Bible study/prayer group. She told me to bring Jasmine and Jessica over to her house early one evening so that her group could "lay hands" on the girls and pray for them. I was really excited because I knew that God used Beverly for the purpose of spiritual healing. (Spiritual healing is divine intervention from God and is also called "faith healing.") God, through Beverly, had healed me (which I will cover later in another chapter), so I just knew that Jasmine and Jessica were getting ready to be healed, in the name of Jesus!

I put them in their highchairs and gave them their dinner. Charles was going to be a little late getting home from work, so I was going to take them by myself. At some point, I went downstairs to the basement to get something. When I came back up the basement steps and tried to turn the doorknob to again enter the kitchen, the door was locked. I shook the doorknob in disbelief. Impossible. No one was home except the girls and me. The girls were in their highchairs, incapable of climbing out, and were distanced several feet away from the door. Geoffrey was at a friend's house, and I had *not* locked the door leading to the basement. I froze. I did not have a key to the door. This was bad. I did not want to miss the opportunity to receive healing for my babies. I could go back down the steps, go through the garage and get to the front door of our house. However, I knew it was locked and my house keys were in the bedroom. The realization hit me. Someone or something did not want this spiritual blessing to take place. I could not let the devil win.

I prayed. Then, with the basement landline phone, I called Charles. He told me where in the toolbox, located in the garage, I could find the correct tool to open the door. He instructed me on what to do and thank God, it worked! I was able to get the door open. The girls were, of course, still sitting in their little highchairs and were fine. I hugged them both, got them ready, and proceeded to Beverly's. When I told her what had happened, she confirmed what I had suspected about "the evil one" trying to destroy our plans. Despite this hurdle, I was relieved and grateful that God had allowed me to get Jasmine and Jessica to this wonderful fellowship of spiritual healing. Unfortunately, although they laid hands on and prayed for the girls, to my dismay, nothing seemed to change.

Some months later, another opportunity for spiritual healing occurred. The building where I was employed housed, on the main level, a dry cleaner. I periodically took clothes there and would talk with the lady who managed the establishment. Her name was Ms. Kim from South Korea, a wonderful person, and a devout Christian. One day, she said, "Mrs. Gray, a faith healer from Africa is visiting our church Friday night. I want you to bring your daughters to the service so that they can be healed." I got the information from her, went home, and told Charles about my conversation with Ms. Kim. Many husbands would have looked at me as if I had three heads, but my husband said, "Okay." So, that Friday evening, we put the kids in the car, dropped Geoffrey off to be with his father that weekend, and then headed to Northern Virginia.

What an experience! We were the only African Americans there, and during the praise and worship portion, all the music was sung in Korean. It was amazing and beautiful to hear the Lord being praised in another language. After the praise and worship, the "healer" was introduced. Another gentleman was assisting him and would select various people from the congregation to come forward. Those who needed healing were told to raise their hands. The music was continuously played and spirits were high. I raised my hands and kept praying that we would be chosen. Finally, we were selected and directed to move into the area near the faith healer. Soon, he came over to us and asked us why we needed healing. Charles and I quickly told him about the girls. He laid his hands on both of their heads and prayed for Jasmine and Jessica. He then took the microphone and put it up to Jasmine's mouth, then Jessica's. He told them to talk, to speak. They babbled just as they normally did. He then said, "I'll be back." His accent almost sounded like Arnold Schwarzenegger's in the movie, *The*

Terminator. The gentleman who was assisting came back to see if the girls were talking. Once he realized that they weren't, he went to interface with others. Neither he nor the faith healer came back to us.

We went home after the service. Although we saw no change in the girls' verbalization, we still had had a great time. It reminded us of the universality of God, that people of so many lands and languages are praising the Lord. Yes, we were disappointed, but we were okay.

I began to question God as to why He had not allowed Jasmine and Jessica to be healed. Charles and I had faith. We believed. We trusted. We were living obedient lives. So, what went wrong? Why did the girls not receive their healing?

Over the years, the Lord taught me more about healing. Yes, He has the power to instantaneously heal. But He also heals over a period of time. Healing can occur through doctors' expertise, procedures and medications. Healing can be spiritual, physical, mental or emotional.

When the girls were about five years old, I watched a very old Christian movie entitled, *The Robe.* It was rare for me to watch movies at that time, as my spare time was indeed, "spare." In this movie, a drunk and disillusioned Roman, Marcellus Gallio (played by Richard Burton, who years ago was a very famous actor), wins Jesus' robe in a dice game after the crucifixion. Marcellus had never been a man of faith like his slave. When his slave escapes with the robe, Marcellus experiences disturbing visions and feels guilty for his actions. Convinced that destroying the robe will cure him, Marcellus sets out to find his slave—and amazingly becomes a Christian along the way. What struck me was a particular scene that pertained to a young, crippled woman. She was sitting on a pallet, smiling and telling people passing by about her Savior, Jesus Christ. Marcellus, prior to his conversion to Christianity, stops to talk with her and asks her about Jesus. He wants to know why, if Jesus was such a healer, didn't He heal her? She replies that

Jesus had healed her soul. Prior to her encounter with Christ, she had been a very bitter person. She was angry that she could not walk, and she had never experienced joy. She also told Marcellus that Jesus could have healed her but did not. Why? She believed that in her crippled state, she could serve Him where she was. She could relate to other people like herself; she could understand how they felt; and she could share the gospel with them. When I watched this scene, I realized that I was on a journey that many other special needs parents travel daily. I was "wearing their shoes," I was living their pain, and I was understanding their circumstances. The television screen became blurry to me as my eyes filled with tears that fell softly down my cheeks. I smiled. I thanked God for blessing me with this revelation.

Another learning experience regarding healing came one day as I sat in my car, in a department store parking lot, getting ready to go inside the store. I was listening to a Christian broadcast, and they began talking about a healing miracle. My ears perked up; I decided to delay my errand and listen to this intriguing story. It was about a minister, Pastor Duane Miller, who was miraculously cured while praying for healing. A simple case of the flu did incredible damage to his vocal cords and his voice sounded like he had a terrible case of laryngitis. He was forced to give up his pastorship and almost lost his faith. Sixty specialists and two hundred doctors could not cure him. His incredible story is still available on the Internet and through the audio link, you can actually hear him trying to teach a Sunday school lesson, which was orchestrated by God. The sermon he gave to the class was on healing. As I listened to this radio broadcast, I could hear his voice change and become stronger. He was instantly healed! This was such an amazing story of healing and restoration. It has now been broadcast and replayed millions of times worldwide. I was so moved that I felt tears well up in my eyes, yet again. God was reminding me, in his gentle loving way, that when it is time for it to occur, He will allow healing to happen. So, I had to keep trusting and keep believing that the blessing of healing would come to my children, someday!

Chapter 5

THE LONG-AWAITED DIAGNOSIS

As I previously mentioned, I gave birth to Jasmine and Jessica, both ways....vaginal and C-section. Not too many women have done this, but I survived. During their labor, I was given an epidural, which is an injection in the back to stop the pain. Nevertheless, I felt Jasmine tumble out of me. Since Jessica had to be removed via emergency C-section, I did not see her being born. Charles was there to witness the entire birthing process. He said that Jessica was very tangled up, compounded by multiple fibroid tumors, which explained why later, the position of her arms and hands were a little "off." Jasmine weighed four pounds, four ounces, and Jessica weighed four pounds, one ounce.

Charles told me that in the Neo-natal Intensive Care Unit (NICU), the girls had IVs and other "wires" connected to them. At one point, the medical personnel even shaved part of Jasmine's hair from her scalp and inserted a sensor connected to a wire. It really bothered him that they did this, but obviously, it was important. These wires enabled the NICU staff to monitor the girls' oxygen, blood pressure, and more. After my sedation wore off, I requested a visit with them. I was wheeled to the NICU, and I finally saw my babies. They were so tiny, adorned with wires and sensors. One day when Charles and Mom were visiting them, they witnessed the insertion of an IV into one of the girls. They both said that when this happened, the other baby flinched—one of the mysteries of twinship.

In the NICU, there were other little infants even smaller than our daughters. In our case, fortunately, neither Jasmine nor Jessica had to be put on a respirator. Thank God they did not encounter any major complications. We were grateful, not knowing that our precious little girls would take us on an unknown and difficult journey.

When Jasmine and Jessica were a month old, it was time to take them for their first doctor's appointment. It was relatively uneventful. However, as time progressed, it became noticeable that they were not developing properly. They were slow doing the things babies normally do, e.g., turning over, sitting up. Sometime after they were 18 months old, with some difficulty, they finally began to walk. It happened one Sunday morning. Jessica pulled herself up and walked down the hallway of our home. We were elated! Jasmine, whose facial expression conveyed that she would not rest until she was walking also, was walking the very next day. Although we were happy that they were now walking, things still were not right with them.

The only health issues they had experienced were periodic ear infections. At each visit to their pediatricians' practice, I kept voicing concern about their delayed speech. Unfortunately, one of their doctors voiced that "they will be fine." Although that was a nice attitude to have, she was mistaken. It would take years to obtain a diagnosis that made sense.

To start with, we insisted that the girls needed to be evaluated at Children's Hospital in Washington DC. The first evaluations were developmental assessments, which determined that they did indeed possess developmental delays. Their hearing was evaluated several times over a five-year period. This was challenging because the girls had difficulty understanding the verbal commands of the audiologists. So, although we knew that they could hear, we did not know *what* they were actually hearing.

Charles and I questioned the girls' developmental delays, investigated our county's Infant and Toddler Program, and got them enrolled in it. A physical therapist and a developmental teacher came to our house and worked with the girls. After they physically improved, more attention was directed to their developmental status. Their speech was underdeveloped, and their comprehension of simple tasks was extremely poor. We were very concerned and tried to understand what was going on with our daughters. However, the real work was just beginning. We needed to help them, but most of all, we needed a diagnosis. What condition or illness did Jasmine and Jessica have?

We were advised to take them to a geneticist for tests at a practice located in a neighboring county. I will never forget that visit. When the doctor gave us his assessment, which was inconclusive, he sat there in his white coat, legs crossed, and told us, "Your daughters don't look like either one of you." I thought to myself, "What is that supposed to mean?" Although there are genetic abnormalities that can occur, both Charles and I were becoming frustrated. Was he right? Deep inside we believed he was wrong. Trust me, our daughters look very much like both of us!

After the Infant and Toddler Program had concluded, it was time for the next phase of the twins' education. With all the medical documentation we had obtained, we sought to enroll Jasmine and Jessica in our county's Special Education program. To begin this process, we had to take them to a school system's developmental doctor. I had to teach a class that day, so Charles took the girls for the evaluation. After all the questions posed to Charles by the doctor, he concluded that the girls had Pervasive Developmental Disorder (PDD), which is viewed as a mild form of Autism. He also told Charles that the girls might never talk and may never be able to effectively communicate. This was truly a difficult assessment to accept. During this conversation, Jessica reached up to her dad, indicating that she wanted him to pick her up. When Charles did so, she proceeded to put her arms around his neck. The doctor was obviously surprised and asked Charles, "So she likes to be held?" Charles answered, "Yes, and she shows affection." Later when Charles and I discussed the assessment and the doctor's question, we knew that he had assumed the girls were

Autistic. Many children with Autism do not like to be held or touched. So, we knew the good doctor was now a little skeptical as to his own diagnosis. Despite his statement, we knew in our hearts that someday, Jasmine and Jessica would be able to talk.

When we continued to voice our concerns about their hearing with the head pediatrician of the practice, he scheduled Jasmine and Jessica to be seen and evaluated by an ear nose and throat (ENT) doctor at Children's Hospital. The girls were now four years old. The ENT doctor detected fluid in both of their ears. He informed us that he would conduct a myringotomy, a procedure wherein he would insert tubes into their middle ears. They were both anesthetized and after the procedure, the doctor told us that there was fluid, resembling jelly, in their middle ears. He suspected that this had always been present. When we asked him how this may have impacted the girls' hearing, he stated, "Pretend you are underwater in a swimming pool. That is probably how they have been hearing." Lord have mercy! This was so upsetting! Both Charles and I believed that this had severely impacted their early development, especially their speech. To this day, we believe this was a factor that crippled their initial years of development.

Over time, we also had other tests conducted. We tried to rule out any unreasonable explanations. Since Jessica's speech was a little more delayed than Jasmine's, Jessica became our "guinea pig" child. We figured if she did not have a particular condition, it was likely Jasmine probably did not have it either. Years later, Jessica was tested for a day and night at Georgetown Hospital to make certain that she had not been having any type of seizures that may have caused her delays. For 24 hours, Jessica underwent a continuous Electroencephalogram (EEG). She had to wear head gear connected with wires that monitored her brain activity. Charles stayed with her during the day. I relieved him after I left work for the day and spent the night in the room with her. This test did not reveal any type of seizure disorder. A few months later, I took the girls to be tested for allergies. The results were inconclusive, no identifiable allergies. Jessica was also tested for heart abnormalities. This test suggested a slight heart murmur, which when tested years later, was discounted. They both experienced breathing difficulties and periodically had to use an albuterol nebulizer. After a few years, this ceased to be a problem and they never had to use it again. Another blessing!

During those early frustrating years, our parental determination and faith in God kept us from faltering. I would read the scriptures posted in their bedroom and ask the Lord, "Will my children ever be able to talk?" One night, I dreamed that Jasmine was talking to me. She spoke a sentence that consisted of five words. When I woke up, I felt that God was showing me that yes, someday, they will be able to talk. That dream gave me comfort, hope and strength to continue to fight for my children's welfare.

Finally, after dealing with improper schooling for our children, we knew we needed to obtain an accurate diagnosis. It was recommended that we take them to Dr. Stephen Mott, who at that time was at Children's Hospital. Because he was an excellent doctor with an incredible reputation, we were placed on a waiting list to see him. Finally, around six or seven months later in 1999, Dr. Mott evaluated Jasmine and Jessica. His assessments included: 1) Encephalopathy, which is damage or disease of the brain that affects language and cognitive development, and 2) Oromotor Dyspraxia, which is an auditory processing condition. We didn't know if the first assessment of encephalopathy was a factor or not. Oromotor Dyspraxia simply means that this disorder makes it difficult to coordinate muscle movements needed to pronounce words. Now this we knew indeed was the case with the girls. If they could not articulate a consonant, they would substitute the correct one with one that they could pronounce. Jessica could not say the "m" sound and would say the "b" sound instead. Until the age of five, instead of calling me "mommy," she called me "bobby." Even today, both

Jasmine and Jessica still have articulation challenges but have come a long way.

Both of the conditions that Dr. Mott identified cause speech and cognitive delays along with distractibility. Even now when talking to Jasmine and Jessica, they need a minute to process what has been said to them and then they need time to respond. They were also easily distracted by other sounds around them. Dr. Mott's diagnosis made so much sense. Now that we had this information, it was time to improve the education and services for our girls. This part of the journey would prove to be a "roller coaster" experience!

Chapter 6

THE IVYMOUNT MIRACLE

The Ivymount portion of our journey was amazing and miraculous! Prior to Dr. Mott's diagnosis, Jasmine and Jessica, as I mentioned before, had significant delays, especially in the area of speech and articulation. Charles and I had voiced our concerns over a three-year period and were assured by their public-school staff that they were "coming along." Their teachers, regarding their speech, kept saying, "The consonants are the last to come." We trusted the school and the Special Education (Ed) team, relying on their expertise when they assured us that the girls were continuing to improve. Each school year, the team consisted of their teacher, an aide, a speech pathologist and the school's Special Ed coordinator. We were cast into the "special needs" world, learning what an Individualized Education Program (IEP) was. This is a document that contains the specialized instruction and services a child with disabilities is to receive. We now attended the IEP meetings and heard educators throw acronyms around like rice being thrown after a wedding ceremony. We had to practically fight to acquire services for the girls, especially in the area of speech development. We expressed our discontent with their curriculum, since much of the curriculum was too difficult for the girls to understand.

Dr. Mott and the speech pathologists at Children's Hospital recommended that Jasmine and Jessica be placed in a small "language-based" environment with at least 45 minutes of speech therapy per day. Encouraged by Dr. Mott's findings, Charles and I initiated a meeting of the IEP team. Despite the diagnosis and the reports we provided, two of their key members questioned the accuracy of our information and stated that they themselves would have the girls tested. Yes, we were a little angry at their questioning, but had no choice but to accept their test pursuit. At our next meeting, they provided the test results, which were almost exactly the same as ours. Yet despite the results, showing how poorly the girls scored in all developmental areas, the team recommended placement for the next school year in one of two "open space" environments. An "open space" setting consists of multiple classes or groups in one physical room. For children with disabilities, especially those easily distracted like Jasmine and Jessica, who needed the exact opposite type of setting, this was absolutely terrible!

Despite our doctor's recommendations, the team allowed only two hours of speech therapy per week. They told us to choose between two schools which they recommended. However, after visiting both schools, we were disappointed and incensed. We couldn't believe that the Special Ed coordinator would even recommend them, especially since she herself had never even visited one of the schools. Unfortunately, we had to choose one of these settings. The better of the schools, which was overcrowded, conducted their two all-day special-ed kindergarten classes physically in the same room, with a partial partition in between. This was a very noisy and distracting environment. It was very difficult for the teachers to teach anything in this setting, including the fact that during the hot months, the school lacked air conditioning.

Much of the curriculum was too complex for our girls. On one particular day, Charles went up to the school with a video camera and visited their classroom. The teacher, using a large paper flip chart, had read them the "Three Billy Goat's Gruff." She instructed the students to help her "diagram the story line." Diagram the story line? Was she serious? Jasmine and Jessica could not even articulate the words "Billy Goat." Charles took out the video camera and began recording this educational fiasco. Someone present must have quickly gone to the principal's office because within minutes, an administrator rushed into the classroom and ordered Charles to leave. Regardless, we got the evidence we needed. We wrote letters, communicating our plight to administrators and Special Education upper-level managers in the county. No one responded. Now desperate, we sought out the superintendent of our school system, who was speaking at a civic meeting held at a nearby school, in hopes that we could speak with her. Her aide kept us from talking to the superintendent directly, but we were able to physically give the aide our envelope containing Jasmine and Jessica's documented situation. Again, we never received a response.

The next school year was even worse. It was another "open space" school and it almost broke my heart. Five classes were in one large room, divided into "pods" (smaller numbers of children) with five-foot-high partitions separating them. You could hear everything that was going on in the other pods. Dr. Mott had told us that Jasmine and Jessica's disability also included "distractibility." Unfortunately, they were placed in one of the pods that contained an inner enclosed office. Much to our dismay, they put the more advanced children, including Jasmine, in the inner office and attempted to teach the other students, including Jessica, in the outer area.

One day I was there to observe and witnessed one little boy just pacing back and forth near where Jessica was sitting. Trust me, very little instruction was taking place. I was so angry that I wanted to scream. Jessica, though unable to tell us how she felt, developed a nervous habit of biting and sucking her bottom lip, which formed a dark line underneath it. Obviously, this environment was very stressful for her. Later, at yet another IEP meeting, we heard the head of the team declare that the girls were fine. By this time, Charles had had enough. He slammed his hand down on the table and declared, "This meeting is over!" He was so very angry, and we immediately walked out. I went to the ladies' room, where my anger overtook me as well. I actually began to cry and my tears felt like hot streams, flowing down my face. I knew that things had to change for our children, soon. I had to believe that God would show us the way.

We did research, finding out that special needs children have the right to a free and appropriate education. If a public school does not or cannot provide an adequate education, our children could attend a private school that could meet their needs. Since the school did not present or offer this alternative, we would need to seek legal advice. We discovered that there were lawyers who represent children with disabilities. We didn't know that this area of law even existed. Again, this journey taught us so much. Debbie, a co-worker of mine and the mother of twins with some "challenges," gave me the names of two highly recommended attorneys. In fact, years later, one of them ended up presenting a case before the Supreme Court. As this particular attorney's calendar was full, we met with another attorney and were blessed to secure him for our legal pursuit.

Our attorney informed us that he would contact the county about our case and was sure that they would finance the education of our children to attend private placement. He instructed us to have the girls evaluated by yet another developmental specialist at a prestigious learning center. The learning center's staff was extremely professional and very nice to us. However, after trying to test Jasmine and Jessica, they found the girls so "challenged," that they only charged us 50% of the cost for Jasmine. Much to our amazement, they put a zero on Jessica's fee slip. Due to Jessica's significant challenges, they were unable to test her, so they did not expect us to pay them. Our poor children! A parent can hardly fathom that their child is so challenged that professionals cannot even "score" them. Devastating! This was remarkably similar to when the audiologists attempted to test the girls' hearing, which was virtually impossible. Our attorney assured us not to worry. He told us that our county had never rejected any of his cases and it was only a matter of time when they would do the right thing. Besides, we had prayed about this, and we knew that God would take care of us.

Soon, our lawyer contacted us. Our county had said no. They would not authorize Jasmine and Jessica to be placed in a private school. He told us that this was the first time that he had ever had a case rejected. That meant that we would have to take the case to court. In all honesty, we just couldn't understand it. "Why Lord, why? Why is this happening?" Since we had obtained a lawyer, this was supposed to be easy. Now we would need to get ready for an upcoming court date. Unbelievable! Yet we still tried to remain positive. We had to keep trusting, believing, and praying.

The Lord heard our prayers. One Sunday morning, we were trying to decide what church to attend. Charles was not a pastor at the time, and we were still visiting different churches. The "little voice" inside me said, "Go to Sargent." So, I told Charles, "Let's go to Sargent Church this morning." Remember, this was my home church, and I accompanied/co-directed the gospel choir on the second Sunday of each month. However, this was not a second Sunday and remember, we usually visited other churches. Charles agreed, and we went. After the service, I went to the nursery to retrieve the girls and found myself, amazingly, sitting next to our state senator. She and her husband were members there, and on this particular Sunday, she was waiting to retrieve her grandchild. Due to our schedules, I had not seen her in quite a while. We exchanged greetings and as we were watching the children play, she asked how our girls were doing. When I told her about our plight, she told me that our situation was unacceptable and gave me the telephone number for one of the members of our county's board of education. She told me to call him as soon as I got home from church and tell him that she wanted a meeting to be set up with our county's school superintendent.

When God answers prayer, He answers prayer! The meeting was set for the following week and consisted of our county's superintendent, the head of Special Education, and us. Dad went with us. No lawyers were included or necessary. We were cautiously excited!

CHARLES REMEMBERS

At the meeting, soon after Arie and I (Charles) exchanged introductions, they tried to have a conversation with Jasmine and Jessica. Now both girls could speak most of the "surface stuff," like "hello" and their names. From there, they could work an entire room and get what they wanted, usually without saying another word. They had adapted to their situation and learned through gestures or pointing how to get their needs met.

So, at the meeting, once the formalities were out of the way, I realized that we had to demonstrate the problem. The Lord, as always when you trust Him, will deliver. Not knowing what to do exactly, I came up with an example I had witnessed earlier at their school. I already knew and had witnessed that our girls were being taught "strategies," as their teachers called them. I called them tricks! This was an example I demonstrated at the meeting. I said, "May I show you a trick?", knowing I had to get them to focus on the word *trick*. The superintendent said, "By all means." Then, I simply asked the girls to say their ABCs, and on queue, both of them started "singing" the ABC song. The singing could be produced simply by saying, "Say your ABCs." I repeated this over and over again. I stated, "This is an example of the tricks both Jasmine and Jessica are being taught across their current learning environment." They did *not* understand the alphabet nor understand its function. Thank you, Lord, for this example, as I could not have come up with a more perfect demonstration that would propel the girls' education forward. Yes, God did it! The head of Special Education again asked them to speak the alphabet. The girls, at age six, couldn't do this and immediately, the enormity of their need was realized. The superintendent instructed the head of Special Education to evaluate the girls' disability documentation and current school setting, and report back to her in two weeks. Two weeks passed. Miraculously, we were called to meet at the Board of Education headquarters to discuss placement for the girls in a private school.

We were ecstatic! Arie and I needed to start visiting private schools to determine which would be an appropriate setting for our daughters. Clay White, one of the Gospel-Aires choir members, had told me about the Ivymount School, which his son had attended. Although located in Rockville, Maryland, in neighboring Montgomery County, quite a distance away, he told me that Ivymount was a great school and that we should try to get the girls enrolled there. He had nothing but praises about Ivymount and compared to other placements, it was a "blue ribbon" school. So after the meeting, I went to the Ivymount School on the following Tuesday. I received a tour of this impressive place. At the end of the tour, I was informed that the cost was approximately $40,000 per year, per child, not including the additional cost of speech therapy. "Oh Lord," I said. "How in the world would we be able to afford all of this?" Trusting God for the answer, I in faith requested two applications. Oh yes, I believed in Hebrews 11:1 "Now faith is the substance of things hoped for, the evidence of things not seen."

ARIE REMEMBERS

The meeting for placement was going to be on a Monday. It was early March, and quite cold. More importantly, the weather prediction was dire. A severe winter storm was forecasted for the Saturday prior to the meeting. By that Friday, its impending severity was going to shut down airports up and down the northeast corridor. How could this happen? The girls' meeting was set, and now we were going to get a snowstorm that would surely cancel everything. The grocery stores even got crowded, as people quickly bought food in preparation for the blizzard.

Miraculously, the snowstorm did not strike us! In fact, it veered east, and incredibly went out to sea. The severe snowstorm prediction was completely wrong, the meeting was not cancelled, and the Lord answered our prayers. The east coast representative who handled "private placement" attended this meeting, which was her last one in the school year for our county. If the storm had occurred as predicted, she would not have met with us until the following school year. She seemed very personable and professional. In fact, the way in which she questioned the county's instructional team regarding our girls' status and what appropriate education was currently being provided, was amazing! To this day, reflecting on her method of questioning the educational team brings smiles to Charles and my faces.

To summarize, she began by complimenting the efforts of the county's instructional team. Charles and I were beginning to become irritated. However, she continued by asking them if they were able to achieve certain fundamental goals and objectives. She was very professional, thorough, and extremely competent! By the time she finished, the team conceded that their school settings did not accomplish Jasmine and Jessica's educational goals. Charles had done most of the leg work, visiting various private schools. We presented the school officials with three of the best possible programs and cited the Ivymount School as our first choice. The east coast representative told us that someone would contact us later as to which school Jasmine and Jessica would attend. The meeting was now over.

We left praising God, singing, and simply giving Him glory. When we got in the car, we laughed, cried, and kept thanking Him for what He had done. Charles called the placement office about a week later to find out if a decision on the school placement had been made. The employee he spoke to reminded him that "this process takes time." He asked her, "Can you just look and see if you have received the paperwork for Jasmine and Jessica Gray?" She still responded that "these things take time." Charles heard her rifling through papers on her desk. He sensed agitation in the nice lady's voice, as she stated that, "If it had come across my desk, I would know it." Then she asked, "What did you say their names were?" He responded, "Jasmine and Jessica Gray." She said, "well, uh...I believe I have their paperwork here. Your authorization is also here. The Ivymount School is your first choice?" Charles said, "That's it. That's where we want them to go." It was done!

Later, when we saw the financial paperwork, that included summer services for the girls, we were stunned. Each year, per child, the cost was thousands of dollars. Our county would incur all of Jasmine and Jessica's educational and travel expenses. We would pay nothing. Nothing! You can imagine, when we contacted our lawyer, how shocked he was to learn what had happened, that we no longer needed his services, and most of all, that the Lord had made this all possible! God had opened every door and the girls were on their way!

Despite our joy, we had concerns. The first concern was the distance. The school was 36 miles away. The traffic in the Washington D.C. metropolitan area can be horrific, especially in the morning. A school bus, having multiple pickups, could easily take 2½ hours one way. But more importantly, we knew no one in the Rockville area. What would happen in the event of an emergency? We needed someone to fill this role, someone who could, if needed, quickly get to Ivymount for us. When God blesses, He is thorough. He supplies all our needs.

A short time before the girls were assigned to Ivymount, our choir, the Sargent Gospel-Aires, gave a concert at Saint Mark Presbyterian Church in (believe it or not) Rockville, Maryland. After that, the church supplied us with a wonderful reception. However, as musicians with equipment to pack up and put away, often, there are either no seats available or the food is

gone. But thank God!   Henrietta, one of our daughters'
godmothers, had saved seats for us, the only seats available,
next to a couple, whom we had never met. They introduced
themselves; we exchanged pleasantries; and they shared a
wonderful health-related testimony of God's healing with us.
Charles and I could tell that they were very nice people, Carol
and Les Henig, a delight to talk with.

Months later, our choir participated in another musical
program at the same church in Rockville. At the reception
following the concert, we spotted the Henigs and proceeded to
greet one another. We discussed with them the girls' diagnosis
and assignment to the Ivymount School. Carol asked if we had
a "backup" plan in the event of an emergency and volunteered
their services. Amazing! They were licensed foster care parents,
and although this was only our second meeting, we could sense
that they were very nice Christian people. They lived within five
minutes of Ivymount. Not only that, but Les said he was familiar
with a disability similar to Jasmine and Jessica's. He proceeded
to share, from an adult perspective, some of the challenges that
can occur. He explained why the girls were easily distracted,
especially in noisy environments. Les told us that when there
are so many different sounds, your brain must determine which
sound is the one you should concentrate on. Incredible! We had
a great time, exchanged contact information, and would
complete the process with Ivymount, enabling the Henigs to be
our emergency points of contact. Charles and I were overcome
with emotion. God had truly blessed us!

Riding home from the concert, I opened my Bible and found
myself viewing Psalm 136. The first verse states, "O give thanks
unto the Lord; for he is good: for his mercy endureth forever." I
could not remember the last time I had read that Psalm. I silently
read it, closed the Bible, and proceeded to engage in
conversation with Charles about what God had done. Dad and
the girls were seated in the back of our van. And then it
happened—another revelation. When we were backing into the

driveway, I turned around in my seat and asked Dad loudly, "Can you believe everything that has happened?" Dad smiled, folded his hands and loudly said, "Thanks to the good Lord. His mercy endureth forever," just out of the blue. I stared back at him in disbelief. He was sitting too far away from me to know the Psalm I had read, nor did I mention just having read it. It was as if my heavenly Father knew what I had read, and then spoke through my earthly father, confirming His word. This became a part of our story, our testimony. When I shared our story with one of Sargent Church's members, she created a beautifully framed picture, which is hanging on one of the walls in our home. It is Psalm 136, adorned with little pictures of the girls and their miraculous journey!

Sometime during early summer, after our unforgettable Rockville concert, the Henigs invited us for dinner, and we had a wonderful time. The more we learned about this special couple, the more we were grateful to the Lord.

September 4, 2001, the morning we had been waiting and praying for, Jasmine and Jessica's first day of school at Ivymount, was finally here! The previous weekend had been very busy and physically, I was exhausted. Jasmine woke up several times that Sunday night, and I didn't sleep well either. Perhaps we were excited but now, this long-awaited day was here at last! We were beyond happy, and I took leave that day from work so that I could experience the first day of the Ivymount miracle. At one point, Charles was helping the girls in the bathroom, brushing their teeth. A few minutes later, I could hear Jasmine singing, on her own, the gospel song our choir sang, "God is a Good God." She had not heard that song in months, yet I heard her singing, in her own verbally challenged yet special way, "He has moved so many mountains, out of my way, God is a wonderful God." My eyes fought back tears of joy!

After photographing pictures of the girls at the house, we helped them board their "little yellow school bus" and, in our car, trailed them to the Ivymount School. We wanted to learn their about their new bus route and simply relish this fantastic experience. What a joy! As we rode along, I could no longer hold back my tears, remembering what we had been through. As their little bus stopped at two houses to pick up other children, I watched their parents, a mother at the first house, a father at the second house, accompanying their children out to the bus. Charles and I now knew some of the struggles that "special needs" parents endure, and although we personally didn't know these parents, we viewed them as comrades. We didn't know how they managed to get their children enrolled in Ivymount, but we had our own story. God had truly blessed us! Yet, we would soon experience another blessing, even in the face of calamity.

Chapter 7

CATASTROPHIC ATTACKS

911

September 11, 2001 started off as a simply gorgeous day. I remember that the air was cool and crisp. The blue sky was eloquently arrayed with fluffy white clouds. My children went to their schools, and I went to work. Geoffrey was in middle school, and Jasmine and Jessica were adjusting nicely to the Ivymount School. They were in the same class, and we were so pleased with their new educational environment. Charles was pursuing his degree in ministry. Since his courses were conducted online, he was at home. God was faithful and again, the Lord was supplying all our financial needs. In quoting an old expression, "all was right with the world."

I was a computer instructor with the Defense Department, located at a military base in Washington, DC. It sits across the Potomac River from the Pentagon, which is actually located in Arlington, Virginia. On this day, I was assisting another instructor, when during our first classroom break, a student, abruptly logged off his computer. He, an army officer, told me that he had to leave our class because a plane had flown into one of the twin towers in New York City! I quickly went to a nearby classroom and told the instructor to turn on the projection system to the television right away. Everyone in the room became silent as we watched the huge screen before us. Smoke was bellowing out of one of the New York tower buildings. In our disbelief, we then saw another plane fly into the other building. We now knew that this was not an accident. I ran out of the classroom, only to see Rob, our local area network (LAN) computer system administrator looking out of the hall window. He said, "There's smoke coming from the Pentagon. Maybe there was some type of crash." I quickly told him what had just happened in New York City and literally ran down the hallway to our office. When I got to my desk, the phone was ringing. It was Charles. Jasmine and Jessica had forgotten their lunches, which he had taken to Ivymount, and he had just passed the Pentagon on his way home. He had pulled over to the side of the road to call me on his cell phone. When I picked up my desk phone, I heard him say, "Get out of your building right away." I immediately grabbed my belongings, and hurriedly told my supervisor that we were under attack and that I was leaving the building. I rushed out the emergency exit door, went down the steps, and out to the front of the building. I was not alone and will never forget seeing others, yards ahead of me, literally running for their lives.

Unfortunately, I realized I had a problem. A couple of months earlier, I had fallen down our outside steps at home and severely sprained my ankle. Although my ankle was better with regular physical therapy, I was still parking in a handicapped space, located in the parking garage *behind* our building. Although I was not an intelligence analyst, nor had been in the military, I was smart enough to know that whoever was attacking us was flying into buildings. To get to my car, I would have to go back into our building, which I had no intention of doing. I spotted a parked cab, rushed over to it and frantically knocked on the driver's window. The cab driver was reading a newspaper and obviously did not even know what was taking place. He rolled his window down and I pointed in the direction of the Pentagon. I told him that we were under attack, and I asked him to take me to my car, which he did. Neither he nor I could understand what was happening. I thanked him, got into my car, and immediately left for home. I found out later that shortly after I left, to ensure security, base police closed the gates and would not let anyone else leave. Fear and shock scarcely describe how I felt. I immediately turned on my car's radio. The announcer was pleading with everyone driving to slow down. He said, "People are running through red lights at intersections!" Yes, folks were panicking. Someone was attacking our country!

Once I got home, which was only ten minutes away, Charles and I hugged each other in disbelief of what was happening. Suddenly, we felt our house, a single-family brick home, vibrate. Later, we found out that the vibrations were coming from explosions at the Pentagon.

We both fell to our knees and began to pray. Now we had to quickly determine how we would get our children home. Geoffrey would not pose a problem, as his school was nearby. But what about the girls all the way in Rockville? The highways had quickly become like crowded parking lots, and the entire Washington D.C area was in a state of panic. Charles wanted to go get the girls but that was now an impossibility. Carol and Les Henig were our only hope. We called Carol, and she said that she would pick up Jasmine and Jessica. The girls would be fine. Why? Because they had just seen Carol and Les on Sunday, two days earlier. What? How did this happen?

It began Sunday morning, September 9th, and Carol was at her kitchen sink. "Something" in her mind told her that they should go and visit Sargent Church. They had never been to our church and out of all the other Sundays, this was the day they chose to attend. Yes, we had seen them at the April concert and had dinner at their house earlier in the summer. But we had not seen them since that time. So, they were obedient to the spirit of God, came to Sargent, and sat with our family, including Dad. Our choir sang that Sunday, and the Henigs got to further bond with the girls. Carol even periodically held each of them on her lap, and we had a wonderful service! This was only our third encounter with them that year, and the most critical encounter of all because now, two days later, Carol would have to get

Jasmine and Jessica from Ivymount. Amazingly, God had prepared our children for that Tuesday, a day that will never be forgotten. Since they had just been with the Henigs at church, Carol was not a stranger to them now. So on September 11th, without hesitation, the girls left Ivymount with Carol. She took them to their home, fed them, and took care of them. Her grandson was also there, and she supplied clothes for them to play "dress up." They had so much fun, playing in and outside. Later that evening, after the roads had cleared from the massive traffic jams that had ensued, Charles was finally able to drive to Rockville. The girls were not eager to come home because they had had such a good time. It was not until many years later that they were able to understand what actually happened on that day.

We will never forget 911. It was the worst terror attack on United States soil in our history. The terrorists had picked September 11th as symbolic, because the numbers for that date, September (9th month), followed by the date of the day, were 911, synonymous with the national phone number for EMERGENCY! Later, we would find out that four planes were hijacked, and thousands of Americans were killed. Since that horrific day, our country has never been the same.

I remember rushing to Geoffrey's school to get him. Other parents had also arrived there to retrieve their children. The atmosphere of panic and shock was overwhelming. While I was waiting in the school's office for them to locate Geoffrey, a student ran into the office and demanded to know what was going on. He was almost hysterical because he knew that something very bad had happened. Understandably, no formal announcement had been given to the students, as no one actually knew what was transpiring. Because I personally knew a couple of the children who had stayed at our neighbor Dolly's home daycare, I called her and got the required permission to bring the children to her house. As Geoffrey, Dolly's kids and I exited the school, helicopters flew overhead, flying in the direction of the Pentagon. Unfortunately, it reminded me of the helicopter scenes in the old television series, *Mash.* Fortunately, Dad was out of town on a senior citizens' bus trip and all of our relatives were accounted for. Many people called us, including my cousin Tommy, as they did not know whether I had been working at the Pentagon on that day. Later, Larry, via phone call, shared words with Geoffrey that I will never forget: "Nephew, our lives will never be the same." How right he was!

Recently, speaking with Geoffrey regarding his account of 911, he recalled things, some of which I knew, some I did not know. I did know that when they called his room for him to report to the school office, he became fearful. That morning, because Ivymount students supplied their own lunches, Charles had left the house before Geoffrey left for school to take the girls' their forgotten lunch boxes. Geoffrey had used the toaster oven to cook something and now that his name was called, he was afraid that he had left the oven on. He was beginning to panic, thinking that our house had burned down. Once there in the office, amidst other parents getting their children, he felt a sense of relief.

What I did not know was that a group of his friends had planned to leave school that morning. They, including Geoffrey, were going to Union Station in D.C., which is a huge transportation hub and shopping center. What a day to skip school, which the group did an hour prior to the plane hitting the first tower in New York! I asked Geoffrey, "Why would you all go there?" He said that they were going to get something to eat at the train station and walk around. Lord have mercy! Fortunately, he felt that his afternoon classes were too important to miss, so he and a couple others did not go with the rest of the group. He told me that he could not even imagine the trauma and fallout that would have occurred if I had gone to the school to retrieve him, only to find out that he was *not* there! In fact, he told me that I probably would have had a heart attack.

Then humorously, he said, "Mom, you would have still had me under punishment."

Another comment Geoffrey made was that some students were outside the school and had actually felt vibrations from the impact of the plane hitting the Pentagon, followed by the explosions. He vividly remembered when we exited his school, seeing the opened side doors of the helicopters flying overhead. He could clearly see soldiers, their uniforms, even the tread of their boots, including the guns they were holding. He knew that something terrible was happening.

On that horrific day, many people throughout the nation lost loved ones. The agency I worked for lost wonderful people at the Pentagon that day, and I knew most of them. Charles lost friends both at the Pentagon and in New York. The trauma and grief remained long after the day passed. Geoffrey remembers that one of his school friends lost his grandmother at the Pentagon. He remembered the car she drove and greetings with her when she was picking up her grandson from Dolly's after school. Yet despite the enormity of September 11th and the grief we all experienced, God supernaturally blessed. So many stories and accounts emanated, and some people experienced their own miraculous rescues. Gratefully, the Lord blessed our family, again! He made a way so that Jasmine and Jessica, in the midst of a catastrophe, were taken care of by the loving couple He had brought into our lives. He protected us all.

THE ANTHRAX ATTACK

As our country, especially the Washington DC area, aka the DMV (District of Columbia, Maryland, and Virginia) was in a state of shock and grief on the heels of 911, another attack emerged: Anthrax. This powder-like substance was mailed to various people and unfortunately, postal workers were the main group exposed to the deadly bacterial agent. Twenty-two people from four areas of our country were exposed and five died. One month after 911, two postal workers in the DMV, who worked for the Brentwood Postal facility in Maryland, lost their lives. Yet again, the entire area now had one more thing to worry about. Our world seemed to be going crazy!

Now we were hesitant about opening our mail. There were some postal shutdowns, and everyone was being very cautious handling what we used to take for granted. We were warned, especially at our places of employment, to be very vigilant in opening mail delivered to our agency. Initially, it was thought to be a continued attack by the perpetrators of 911. But years later, an employee at Fort Detrick Maryland was thought to have been involved. This was never completely determined, and no one was ever prosecuted. God again protected our family.

THE BELTWAY SNIPERS

In that first year at Ivymount, Jasmine and Jessica were placed in the same class. Their main teacher was excellent, as she also taught using "sign language." The girls began to improve, and we were again thankful for them being at this wonderful school. However, we were advised, for their second year, to have them placed into separate classrooms. We agreed. Jessica tended to "lean on" Jasmine, especially in the area of communication. Even today, if you ask Jessica a question, often, she will visually look at Jasmine. Twins often do this, but they both needed to become more independent. Separate classrooms would also allow them to develop their own classmate relationships. They adjusted better than we expected and really seemed comfortable in their school setting.

On October 2nd, we heard on the local news that a man was shot and killed in Montgomery County where Ivymount is located. Little did we know that soon, yet again, our lives would turn upside down. Our country, especially the DMV, was still reeling from the events of 911. During that previous month of September, we had just commemorated the one-year anniversary of that terrible day. Many of us were captured by the televised heartbreaking tributes made to the many victims of 911. We watched the emotional roll call of names broadcast from New York. We viewed the ceremonies that took place at the Pentagon and Pennsylvania. The phrase "let's roll" became an example of such bravery, exemplified by the brave souls who fought the terrorists on that fateful flight near Shanksville, Pennsylvania. It was believed that the hijackers intended to fly that plane into the White House or the U.S. Capitol. My agency, the Defense Intelligence Agency, had its own memorial service dedicated to its employees killed at the Pentagon. As I often sang at many of our agency's events, I was asked to sing the National Anthem for this service. Though fighting back tears, I focused on the flag and sang to the best of my ability. I had to deliver the anthem amidst the presence of the family members, co-workers, and friends of those dear people who were tragically killed. In a bizarre way, the healing process that began with 911 would soon be greatly impaired.

On October 3rd, the day began, as it did on 911, uneventfully. Our children were at school, Charles was home continuing his ministerial courses online, and I was at work. Soon, my co-workers and I were alerted that people in different locations were being shot in Rockville, Maryland. Charles also called me to let me know what was going on. I wasn't teaching that day and was working at my desk when I got a phone call from Geoffrey. For safety reasons, especially after 911, we had given him a cell phone to use only for emergencies. He had gone to a school restroom to call me, and I could hear the desperation in his voice. "Mom, what's goin on? What about Jasmine and Jessica?" I told him that I had just called the school and that they were under lockdown. I told him not to worry, return to his class, and wait for any instructions that the school would communicate. As a mother, it broke my heart that he was compelled to make that call to me. What was the world coming to? Unbelievable!

Unfortunately, Jessica's class was in D.C. for a field trip. When I remembered this, I called the school again. They told me that Jessica's teachers had been notified and that they were on their way back to Ivymount. All we could do was pray. Thank God that our children returned home safely that day. However, Jessica's behavior was different that afternoon. She has always been very sensitive and can sense the emotions of others around her. We could only imagine what her day had consisted of. Her field trip was interrupted. They must have arrived at the museum only to immediately turn back to Ivymount. There was obviously a huge police presence, including helicopters flying above the entire Rockville area. The school personnel on the field trip had to have facially shown some degree of concern. Once back at the school, they were in a lockdown situation. Jessica looked sad when she came into the house and immediately went to her dad for a hug. We could sense that she wanted to be held, so as we sat in the living room, Charles held her in his lap. Lord have mercy!

The sniper attacks continued. Law enforcement realized that on October 2nd, the shooting of a man in a parking lot in Wheaton, Maryland, was the beginning of the carnage that had begun. The entire DMV was traumatized. Randomly, people were shot and killed in Maryland, DC, and Northern Virginia. One victim was simply buying gas. Another person was leaving a store, and one lady was sitting at a bus stop. The fear we experienced was similar to that felt on 911 but this time, it was much more personal. Whenever we left our home, we moved quickly and constantly looked over our shoulders. A police report was issued to look out for a white van or box truck. Each time we spotted this type of vehicle, we immediately took cover and hoped that we were not noticed by the sniper. Even simple tasks, such as going to the grocery store, were impacted. People would buy their groceries, literally run to their cars, throw their grocery bags inside their vehicles, and quickly leave the premises. I'm sure there were many instances of broken eggs that didn't survive this type of treatment.

Many were even afraid to buy gas, as most stations were now self-service. When pumping gas, people crouched behind their cars and nervously looked around at their surroundings. Charles usually took care of this. Yet I remember at least once or twice having to purchase it. Only those who lived through this can understand how it felt to kneel down trying to pump gas and simultaneously protect your body from a phantom shooter. Also, most if not all outdoor events were cancelled, including school football games.

Another simple activity impacted was our children's outside play time. I remember only one instance when I allowed them to play in our backyard. I, a little tense, sat in a chair on the patio. During the entire *five* minutes, I surveyed our surroundings, peering as best as I could through the trees. It was crazy. Looking back on it, did I really think that I could have spotted the sniper, especially in time to save us? I didn't want the children to know how bad this really was. For their sakes, I tried to act as if everything was fine, but was relieved only after we safely got back inside the house.

On the morning of October 7th, a 13-year-old boy was shot in front of his school in Bowie, Maryland. Now the bad dream had become a nightmare. Every parent in the area was afraid and deeply concerned about the safety of their children. Teenagers and children were petrified. Adults being killed was bad enough, but this was horrific. This monster had now shot a child, proving that he didn't care if he killed children. This was too much!

At the news conference held by law enforcement, Chief Charles Moose, who at the time was the Montgomery County Maryland chief of police, gave an emotional plea for the capture of this villain. As tears rolled down his face, we as parents were also distraught. No more letting our children play outside. We had to determine whether it was safe for our kids to even go to school. Some briefly kept their children at home. No one felt safe! Geoffrey said he felt okay at school because his school was surrounded by trees. Little did he know that when I told my co-worker Jacki what he had said, she responded with "Arie, you can see his school from Highway 210." I did not tell Geoffrey, as I did not want him to be afraid. This was a fact he did not need to know.

The victims of the shootings were doing normal day-to-day activities, like the father who had just left a grocery store after buying snacks for his son's church youth group. This three-week-old nightmare resulted in 10 people killed and three injured, including the 13-year-old boy. These people were innocent victims of evil, pure and simple. They consisted of various races, sexes and now, ages, young and old. It was as if the entire DMV was living a nightmare and couldn't wake up.

The snipers began communicating with the police. They left behind tarot cards, taunted law enforcement, and referred to themselves as "God." Since most of the shootings had taken place in Rockville, Charles and I questioned whether we should pull the girls temporarily out of school. Now that the young student was shot in our own county, we also questioned Geoffrey's safety. We prayed about it, and the Lord gave us a sense of peace that He would protect Geoffrey and the girls. In Mark Ward's book *Shots In The Dark: The Sniper, The Suburbs and The Things We Value Most*, which was written from a Christian perspective, he discussed various victims of the shootings. One victim, in particular, was given one of the best eulogies a man could receive and many at his funeral, including his pastor, questioned why someone so full of life had to die like that. It was a question asked by all those touched by the ten tragic deaths of October 2002. Mark Ward also cited that the victim's brother spoke at the service and recounted his brother's life, including the fact that his brother had experienced the sudden death of his wife who was killed two years earlier in a car accident. Despite his brother's struggle with anger and bitterness, he decided to trust God. Yes, that was now the real issue for all of us and so that is what we had to do. It was the best solution, the only solution, covered with prayer. We knew that many people were praying for all of this madness to cease!

God answered our prayers. After a few weeks into this calamity, the snipers began making careless mistakes. The FBI and law enforcement were able to determine the correct vehicle description, which was actually a blue Chevrolet Caprice. The news media quickly released this information and later, on the night of October 23rd, we watched news coverage in anticipation, as sightings of the vehicle had been reported. Finally, in the early morning hours of October 24th, the snipers, John Allen Muhammad and Lee Boyd Malvo, were captured and arrested. The entire DMV breathed a collective sigh of relief. Unbelievably, these two men, prior to the murders in the DMV, had killed a few people in several other states. The lead sniper was convicted and executed on November 10, 2009. The other sniper, who was a juvenile at the time, is serving multiple life sentences. We prayed for the families devastated by 911, the families affected by the anthrax scare, and now the families impacted by the snipers, that God would grant them the strength needed to go on. We were grateful that once again, the Lord had blessed us by protecting us from danger and harm.

* * * * * *

Geoffrey will now share some of his memories
in the next chapter.

Chapter 8

GEOFFREY REMEMBERS

I remember occasions when my parents seemed to have special help from God. Almost all the time, they seemed to be one step ahead of me. Here are a few of those memories.

THESE GLASSES

I had these gold rimmed glasses that I loved for about five minutes after my mom and I left an optical store in Iverson Mall Shopping Center. If you're unfamiliar with Iverson Mall, which is in Oxon Hill, Maryland, during the early 2000s, it was a fairly decent mall. In my opinion, it had the best cookie shop in the entire area. If I had been well behaved and kept my grades up, Snicker Doodles were my treat!

Back to the glasses. Clayton Drive in Oxon Hill is the place where I grew up. Our street was a back street, yet served as one of two ways to get to Potomac High School. My friends and I preferred to ride our bikes or play ball in the street. This was a difficult task on Clayton because of the traffic, so we played around the corner on Leland Drive. Leland was a dead-end street that intersected Clayton.

This is where it gets weird. I was walking with my friends down on Leland Drive after coming from the "candy lady," who sold snacks to us kids in the neighborhood. She was a very nice person, and trust me, she had been thoroughly vetted by my mom. On this particular day, I had a very dumb thought. I would act like I lost my glasses while I was riding my bike. That was the dumb thought. Looking back on it, I wasn't even good at

destroying evidence. I literally put them down right near the
street gutter and continued to walk down the street. I felt free. I
thought, "Now I can get some glasses I actually won't regret
choosing, with Mom's money of course.

Fast forward to that evening. I had it all planned out. I'd tell
Mom I had lost my glasses. Risking her to become angry and/or
grounding me seemed worth it at the time. Finally at some point
that evening, I mustered up the courage to tell my lie. I could
tell that she did not believe it at all. Then, I tried another tactic,
which was to blame Jasmine and Jessica, who were little girls
at the time. I told Mom that they must have hidden my glasses
somewhere. Of course, that made no sense. Finally, I stated the
most ridiculous theory that had ever exited my mouth and said,
"A ghost must have taken them." That's right. I had the nerve
to say that to my mother with a straight face. Little did I know
what was waiting just ahead. After telling these ridiculous lies
to my mother's face, she pulled a magic trick unlike any that I
had ever seen. "So the ghost took these glasses?" she asked as
she pulled the glasses out of her jacket pocket. You could've
swept my mouth off the floor.

How? How did she find them? Here is my mom's account: "I
rarely ever traveled up Leland Drive for anything. On that day,
all I knew is that "the little voice" told me to drive up that street.
I thought I was being led to do so, just to see the houses and
spot any changes to our neighborhood. As I slowly drove along,
something caught my eye. It was shiny and lying near the street
gutter. I stopped the car, walked over, and to my surprise, the
shiny thing was Geoffrey's eyeglasses, reflecting the sunlight. I
picked them up, inspected them to determine if they were
damaged, which they weren't, and returned to the car. I thought
to myself, 'Why were his glasses here?' It was a miracle that
they had not fallen into the street. They were still intact. I
carefully put them in my jacket pocket.

When Geoffrey got home a short time later, I thought he
would tell me what had happened to his eyeglasses. He said

nothing, and I decided to wait to see how long this situation would go on. Finally, he began telling his series of lies. I was very disappointed in him and of course, enacted some form of punishment. One thing I remember telling him was that God had directed me to drive up Leland that day and that He helps us, as parents, care for our children. Years later, we laughed about this episode, especially that he blamed his sisters, followed by the ghost theory. Yes, we often forget that God also has a sense of humor!"

BACON, EGG, CHEESE AND EMBARRASSMENT

Occasionally, my closest school friends would get up early and head to the metro bus stop before school started. We would catch the P12 bus toward Iverson Mall. Before we got to Iverson, there was a small strip mall that included a Popeyes, a Safeway grocery store, a McDonald's, and a few other businesses. This was a unique McDonald's with no drive-through since it was smack dab in the middle of the strip mall.

I was a huge fan of anything bacon, egg and cheese. On a biscuit was my preference. I placed my order among 20 other of my fellow Shugart Junior High School students. While I was waiting for my food, I got a tap on my shoulder. "Isn't that your dad?" one of my friends asked. In a big burgundy Ford truck outside the window was, you guessed it, my dad. "Why was he here?" was the question going through my mind. Even worse, my order number was being called but I had to ignore it. I walked outside to the truck, hopped in, and started with "Hey Dad."

"Geoffrey, why are you up here?" he asked. Now usually I would have a better answer than what I'm about to tell you *but*, I was hungry, and my mental sharpeners were indeed off. "Because I was hungry," was what my peanut-sized brain came up with to say. Then, in a low and patient tone Dad said, "We have food at home. I don't want to catch you coming up here anymore. We're clear?" he asked.

"We're clear," I softly replied. Now, let me remind you. This McDonald's is in a strip mall. Ninety percent of the front of the building is glass windows. Behind those windows were about 20 pairs of eyes staring out. Some faces were in horror, others were smirking or laughing. As the truck backed up and Dad drove me the rest of the way to school, I was thinking, "Man, I wonder who got my bacon, egg and cheese biscuit because that's probably the last time I'll be at McDonald's for a while." Why was he there? Here is my dad's account: "The only remembrance of why I drove up to the McDonald's that morning was that something led me to go there. Once there, it quickly became apparent, as Geoffrey came out the McDonald's door and got into the truck. He later told me that he never did that again."

TURN THE VAN AROUND

I was in high school and had just gotten my driver's license. It was one of, if not the biggest, milestone for me at that point of my life. Ever since I was a toddler, driving was something I'd always wanted to do. No really, there are pictures of me in our family photo albums driving a toy car at around four years old. In my mind, getting my license was a necessity.

I had heard about a party earlier in the day and knew this was my chance to show off my driving skills to my friends. Mom had a Honda Odyssey minivan. Nothing special but it was definitely a nice van. I told my friends that I would come pick them up one by one and then head to the party.

My dilemma was that I didn't know the exact address of the party, but my friends knew how to get there. This was before smart phones. Printing out Mapquest pages was still "a thing." The problem I ran into was my mother's curiosity. When she asked where the party was, I told her at the house of a kid named Craig. Craig was one of the people whom I was picking up. He also knew where the party was going to be. I called Craig on the house phone, yes the house phone, and told him that I was on the way. Looking back on it, we should've talked on my cell phone, but its reception was bad in my bedroom. So, I told Mom where I was headed and off I went, with a curfew of course.

One by one, I picked up my friends, about four of them if memory serves correctly. At last, I reached Craig's house! Almost to the party! As I'm rounding the cul-de-sac, I get a phone call. "Turn the van around," were the first words I remember hearing, which came from my mother's mouth. No way she had found out the party wasn't at Craig's house. Well, of course she did indeed find out my *lie*. She had called Craig's house number using our caller ID and had asked to speak to one of Craig's parents, to verify the party. His dad had answered the phone and of course stated that they were *not* hosting a party. The rest is "history."

The most embarrassing part wasn't driving my friends back home one by one within a half hour of just picking them up. No, the most embarrassing part was having my license taken away for over six months. I'll never forget that feeling.

After that, I learned to just tell the truth with no regrets. I'm glad these incidents occurred, which were actually blessings in disguise. Without them, I'd probably still be throwing my glasses off the P12 bus on my way to McDonald's for a bacon, egg and cheese biscuit.

Geoffrey and His Glasses

Chapter 9

A SCHOOL BUS DILEMMA

When the girls were about nine years old, we experienced a potentially dangerous school bus situation. In addition to paying for our girls' education at Ivymount, our county also provided their transportation to school. To ensure safety, when special needs children ride school buses, especially those who are young, the driver is required to wait until the children are received by a parent or caregiver.

One day, Dennis, our choir's drummer, stopped by our house. While he and Charles were conversing in the living room, the girls' school bus came. When Charles got to the door, the bus was gone. The driver had not waited for him to even get to the door. The girls were outside alone, standing beside the street. He was quite upset about this and when he tried to talk to the bus driver the following morning, she became defensive and rude. We had no other recourse but to immediately report her. Charles tried to meet with her supervisor to no avail and made multiple phone calls. Finally, we were told to submit paperwork to the county's school transportation office. Instead of mailing it, I decided to take it there personally in hopes that I would meet the supervisor. Once at the office, I was told that (let's call her *Ms. Jones*) was not there and since she was at an appointment, out of the building, they didn't know if she would return later that Friday afternoon. I placed the envelope containing our information on her desk and headed home.

The following Monday was chaotic throughout the entire metropolitan area. We had a substantial rainstorm and trust me, the road conditions were very challenging, to say the least.

I had an early morning errand at our doctor's office and from there, continued my commute to work. For some interesting reason, I had a desire to buy some coffee. I exited my route and decided to go to a nearby 7-Eleven. A little voice said to me in my mind, "Go to Starbucks" which was also nearby. But I answered the little voice, "Starbucks is more expensive than 7-Eleven." I further rationalized that the 7-Eleven was also more convenient, as it was on the right side of the road. Starbucks was on the left side of the dual-laned roadway. The little voice again said, "Go to Starbucks." So, I obediently did. It was very crowded, and I found myself standing next to a lady who was also waiting to order coffee. I noticed that she was holding an AKA (Alpha Kappa Alpha) Sorority keychain. Since I was also a member of that sorority, I struck up a conversation with her. She seemed very nice, and I enjoyed our impromptu time together.

A few minutes later, we paid for our coffees, and she went over to the side to wait until they called her number. While I was also waiting for my number to be called, the "little voice" told me to go over to her to exchange names. So, I went over and introduced myself to her and then she introduced herself to me. Yes, you guessed it. Incredibly, she was the transportation supervisor whom we were trying to meet with! That's right, this was Ms. Jones, the person on whose desk I had left the bus information on that previous Friday. I was so shocked, that I could hardly say the words, "I'm Jasmine and Jessica Gray's mother." We both stared at each other in disbelief. I then said, "Oh my God". Then she quietly said, "Let's go over here to a table and talk." Can you imagine how amazed I was that God had put this together? With all the weather conditions, with all the disorder in the area, with all the traffic delays, during all of this, God arranged this meeting. We both agreed that only He could have done this. Ms. Jones was very kind and professional. She told me that we would get this all worked out.

After our "meeting," I got into my car and called Charles in tears, laughing and crying at the same time. He was astounded as well. Only God! When I got to my desk at work, I was almost giddy, and I could not hide my excitement. One of my co-workers, who considered herself an atheist, came over to my desk to find out what was going on. When I told her what had happened, she stared at me and replied, "Arie, you're giving me chills." I could tell by the look on her face that she was greatly affected by my story. Although she didn't say it, I knew that even she knew, that only God could have orchestrated this outcome!

Days later, we were to have a meeting, including the bus driver (let's call her *Ms. Karen)*, Ms. Jones, and the head of transportation. Charles and I went to the meeting, only to find out that Ms. Karen was not there. Someone probably advised her not to attend. We were angry, and I was downright mad! I had used valuable leave hours from my job, so this certainly did *not* sit well with me. The head of transportation apologized and told us that a few months ago, Ms. Karen had lost her mother. She was also dealing with other family issues, but those circumstances did not excuse her behavior.

The next day, Ms. Karen was officially removed from being the girls' driver and transferred to another route. Other drivers filled her vacancy. However, I couldn't help but notice that their demeanors seemed a little "cool" toward me when I would greet them as they dropped off the girls in the afternoons. I told Charles about this, but he replied, "As long as they do what they are supposed to do, we can ignore this." He was right of course, and I did just that!

After each regular school year concluded, Jasmine and Jessica received summer instruction at Ivymount. Much to my dismay, Ms. Karen was back and had resumed being their bus driver. I called the head of transportation to express my feelings, but he said that despite what had happened earlier in the school year, she was an excellent driver, and they were short of drivers who were trained to transport special needs students. He told me that if we experienced any additional problems to let him know. I was upset at first but the Christ in me led me, the next day, to walk out to the bus. I spoke to Ms. Karen and asked, "May I talk to you for a minute?" She agreed so I got on the bus and proceeded to tell her that I had been told her mother had passed. I told her that I was very sorry and that I understood. Summarizing what had happened to me, she now knew that we had both experienced similar griefs. I could tell, as she talked about missing her mother, that it saddened her. Believe it or not, I gave her a hug. I also gave her some encouragement and told her that the Lord would help her, just as He had helped me. "Grieving is a process. I will be praying for you," I said. Not only was she very appreciative, but she promised me that she would always look out for Jasmine and Jessica. From that point on, we had a very good relationship. The girls loved her, and we never encountered any more problems.

It was a lesson in the supernatural provisions, an incredible example of His divine blessings. Through a rainstorm and chaos, God navigated the meeting with Ms. Jones, which was nothing short of a miracle. The Lord also provided another opportunity for me to remember the power of forgiveness and to experience the blessings that came from trusting Him. To God be the glory!

Chapter 10

HEALTH ISSUES – GOOD GRIEF!

Charlie Brown would often say in the Peanuts world, "GOOD GRIEF! That's the way I felt over the years, dealing with health issues. Although I escaped a rear-end collision on the day Charles and I were married, unfortunately over the years, I have had *eight* car accidents. It was as if people just viewed me as a target, a bullseye, and would run into me. Each accident was the fault of the other driver and most of them ran into the back of my vehicle. Because I have scoliosis, which is a curvature of the spine, each accident severely sprained my neck, back, or both.

One of the accidents was different than the others and could have been deadly. It was the Saturday before one of our choir's anniversary concerts. We had just finished rehearsing and now stood in a circle with one another, holding hands and closing with a prayer. I was standing in between Charles and Larry, who was a member of the choir at that time. Hours later, Larry told me that as we were praying, he was thinking "I'm remembering what her hand feels like." Little did we know what would happen fifteen minutes later.

We were all so excited, looking forward to our concert! Because of this "jam packed day," Charles and I had driven to the church in separate vehicles. He was headed to a family reception, and after dropping off the children at the sitter's house, I would join him there. While we were travelling on Interstate 295, I noticed a large truck in front of me with a lot of items that later proved to be unsecured. Suddenly, one of the truck's objects was ejected into the air. It appeared to be part of a huge wood and metal crate. As it flew in a circular direction through the air, it resembled Dorothy's house in the *Wizard of Oz* movie. The crate was heading toward us so quickly that I had no time to take evasive action. It slammed down onto the front of the top of the car, barely missing the windshield by no more than an inch. "Bam!" The noise of the impact was almost deafening. I was in shock yet maintained control of our vehicle. Thankfully, when the crate bounced off the roof, it landed safely onto the shoulder of the highway. Damage was done to our car and only by God's grace, were we not harmed. Later when I called Larry to tell him what had happened, he told me about holding my hand in the prayer circle and how he had a premonition that something bad was about to happen. I knew then that we were not just lucky, as some would say. We were blessed!

I always knew that God was a healer and that He cares about every aspect of our lives, including our health. Throughout my life, I have learned about spiritual healing (discussed in Chapter 4) and spiritual warfare. Spiritual warfare is fighting against evil forces that try to attack us. The Lord has always blessed me with spiritual warriors where I was employed, and those wonderful saints have helped me as I experience this journey called life. Beverly, my main prayer partner, had such a sweet spirit and was such a blessing to me. She told me that my being injured resulting from so many car accidents was the work of the enemy. She conveyed to me that God, through His grace, had prevented me from serious injury or death.

As I stated previously, Beverly had the spiritual gift of healing. I experienced this gift more than once, but one time, it was truly amazing! Prior to Charles and I meeting one another, Geoffrey, Mom, Dad, and I had gone to Busch Gardens in Williamsburg, Virginia. We were getting ready to leave the amusement park and Dad proceeded to start the car. He immediately put the windows down to let out the hot air that had built up during the day. He didn't realize that I was reaching into the car to retrieve something and began putting the windows back up. The window I was reaching through quickly began to close on my upper arm. I started screaming, as did Mom, and Dad finally pushed the window button down. Unfortunately, the damage was done. My arm was not only hurting, but my hand and fingers were now numb. This continued for the rest of the evening and into Monday, the next day.

I went to work, knowing that I needed to make an appointment with my doctor. But thanks be to God, I located Beverly. I told her what had happened, and she arranged for us to meet in a quiet location inside our building. She laid hands on my upper arm, and I felt movement! As she prayed, my arm bulged and again, I felt tingling inside the injured area. She said to me "Arie, you had a lot of damage." I was amazed! After it was over, all the feelings in my arm, hand and fingers returned. I was so overwhelmed and grateful at the same time. She told me to get a small ball or something to squeeze to help get my strength back to normal. Glory to God, I did not have to go to the doctor because I had been healed through the power of Jesus Christ! My strength was also restored.

There were other times I called Beverly for prayer and healing. Usually, right before the choir's anniversary concert, I would either fall ill or lose my voice. But God always prevailed, and on those occasions when Beverly and others prayed for me, the Lord healed me. With each solo I sang, I gave God the glory He deserved!

After having the girls, unfortunately, I continued to have high blood pressure issues and, of course, back and neck problems from all the car accidents. My last car accident led to cervical surgery in early 2000 and to this day, I have a metal plate in the neck portion of my spine. The surgery was done by going in through the front of my neck, incorporating bone from a bone bank, and ultimately fusing the discs. The surgeon had advised

Charles and me that during the operation, my vocal cords would have to be temporarily moved. He also said that I also faced the possibility of permanent hoarseness. For over two years, I had suffered immense pain and loss of mobility. I had tried virtually every means of treatment, but nothing had worked. So, despite the risks, I again had no choice but to trust God...that after the operation, He would enable me to talk and sing his praises.

Within a couple of days after returning home from the hospital, I began experiencing excruciating pain. It felt like I was having severe muscle spasms at the sight of the incision. They almost felt like the contractions a woman feels during labor, giving birth to a baby. The pain was so bad that Charles contacted the doctor, who told him to take me back to the hospital. I was admitted yet again and they began running tests to find out what was wrong with me. At one point, the medical team came into the room to assess my situation. I moaned as one of the pain episodes struck my neck. A hospital doctor looked down at me and said, "Mrs. Gray, try to contain your pain." He seemed so uncaring, showing no compassion for my dilemma. I will never forget how angry his remark made me. I was in so much pain that I could barely speak. Fortunately, they gave me stronger pain medication and monitored my status.

The second evening of this hospital stay, after eating dinner, I was taken to another floor to receive an MRI. Once the technician did his initial preparation, I was soon inserted into the MRI machine. I lay there, with my neck completely adorned with surgical dressings, trying to keep still as I had been instructed. Unfortunately, a big problem emerged. I began to regurgitate the recent food I had eaten. Something that felt like hot acid started coming up from my chest. Desperately, I pressed the "help" button so that I could come out of the machine. Nothing happened. I repeatedly pressed the button, only to receive silence. Due to the surgery, I could not scream, yell, or talk above a whisper. I was belted on the pallet table and could scarcely move. Lying there moaning for help, tears slowly rolled from my eyes. I was trapped and felt like I was lying in a tomb. I realized I could choke on the vomit that was slowly coming up in the direction of my neck and that only God knew what was going on. I couldn't die like this. Charles was not there to save me, and the technician had obviously left the room. "Jesus, please save me," I silently prayed.

Just as the burning liquid was coming up into my throat, I felt myself moving out of the machine. Thank God! The technician, seemingly unaware of what was going on with me, had finally rolled me out. He then tried to prepare me for the second part of the test. I told him to stop and let me sit up right away to keep from choking. He did so and after a minute, I said, "You left me in there and I could have choked to death." I painfully stated, "This test is over. Take me back to my room, now!" and he complied. I thanked God that He prevented me from choking to death. I soon was discharged and went home.

The painful attacks continued, but yet again, God blessed. April, a Sargent Church member, called to check on me. Due to the pain medications, I was asleep, so Charles spoke with her. He explained what was happening to me, and she revealed that she had experienced a very similar situation. She said that her unexplainable pain was caused from the abrupt removal of her muscle relaxant after her surgery. Charles realized that after the surgery, I should have been administered the muscle relaxant that I had been taking for over two years. My body had become dependent on this medication. Now that I was no longer taking it, severe muscle spasms in the location of my surgical incision had resulted. Once this was corrected, I was soon on the road to recovery. Thank God for the revelation He gave to Charles! I could not recall April ever calling me, as our conversations only occurred at church. So, for her to call me was indeed a blessing from the Lord! Later, I wrote a letter to the hospital to express my sentiments with the "unfeeling" doctor. I also prayed that someday, he would realize his mistake and become more caring to his patients.

Praise God, despite the moving of my vocal cords, I can still sing and some years ago, recorded a gospel music CD entitled "Miracle of Love." Jasmine and Jessica even sang background vocals on one of the selections I wrote, entitled, "A Father's Love." A few of my experiences, especially influenced by my "labor of love," are reflected in a couple of the selections. For instance, near the end of the song "Miracle Of Love," I sing the words, "When I almost lost my mind, you were there." This refers to the night I wanted to end my life. I am so grateful that the Lord gave me the opportunity to write some of the songs, which reflected my testimony.... my journey, our journey.

One evening, sometime later, I unexpectedly experienced shortness of breath and chest pain. Was I having a heart attack? Charles called 911. I was put into an ambulance, and as they proceeded to take me to the hospital, they tried to insert an IV. Unbelievably, they had not secured the ambulance doors. Within three minutes after leaving our house, the back doors of the ambulance flung open. There I was, looking at traffic right behind us, waiting for the stretcher I was lying on to fly out of the ambulance. I don't want to visualize what could have happened next. Fortunately, one of the EMT's grabbed the stretcher to keep me from rolling out of the ambulance and probably becoming an accident casualty. I felt like I was acting out a scene from a television show. Incredible!

After an overnight hospital stay, they could not find any evidence of a heart attack but advised me to see a doctor. After being tested, a pulmonologist, Dr. Armstrong, informed me that I had asthma. I was very surprised and upset but hoped that I would be alright. He assured me that with medication and good personal care, I would be fine. Asthma often occurs to long-time allergy sufferers, which I was.

I am blessed that I have had very few asthma attacks. In fact, during my life, the Lord has guided me through the two significant attacks that have occurred. One time I had some type of upper respiratory infection. I was at my job, working at my desk, and suddenly started coughing. I then had an asthma attack! I had never experienced this before, but I recognized what it was. I grabbed an albuterol inhalant, which I always carried with me, took the prescribed puffs, and immediately called my primary care physician's office. The staff member could tell that I was upset and still having some breathing difficulty. A nurse got on the phone and spoke with me. She coached me through the episode, and kept saying "Mrs. Gray, breathe slowly. Breathe slowly." I complied and it finally subsided. She then told me to come in for a treatment, which I did later that afternoon. I felt a little better and went home.

However, later I felt worse again and started having another attack. Charles was not at home, and I was sitting at the foot of our bed. The next thing I knew, Jasmine, who was probably about eight years old, came into the room, sat down next to me, and said, "Mommy, breathe slowly. Breathe slowly." Not only did I obey her, I knew that God had to be speaking through her. First of all, her speech was very challenged. Secondly, neither she nor her sister used adverbs like the word "slowly." But most of all, I had not told anyone about what the nurse had said to me about breathing slowly. How did she know this? Only God, the nurse, and I knew about that conversation. The Lord used my child to help me in this hour of need.

The other significant episode was more critical, and not having my inhaler with me, could have proven deadly. I was at Reagan National Airport in Washington DC., preparing to fly to Fort Bragg, North Carolina, to teach a computer class. While I was waiting for my flight, I realized that I had left my small pouch containing my asthma inhalant on the front seat of our car. Charles had dropped me off, so I immediately called him to return. Unfortunately, he did not hear his phone. Initially, I didn't think it would be problematic, as I seldom experienced asthma attacks. By this time, I had not had one for quite a few years. However, I felt a sense of uneasiness. It was as if something was urging me to get my inhaler. Then Lucille, one of my friends, happened to call me to chat and when I told her what was going on, she reminded me that I could go to a CVS drug store upon reaching my destination. I could have my prescription filled there. That seemed like a great plan and once I landed in North Carolina and got into my rental car, the urging commenced again. It made me seek out a CVS and once I explained my situation to the pharmacist, they easily filled my prescription for the inhalant. I immediately felt a sense of relief.

Later that day, and during the following days, I found myself having to teach in a very dusty room, with computers that had been used in Iraq. This was during the springtime and pollen was everywhere. A light, green-colored dust covered the cars and virtually everything in sight. Not realizing it at the time, a perfect storm was about to occur. After the class concluded on that Friday morning, I left for home. The flight plan, going there and returning, took me through Charlotte, North Carolina. Unfortunately, there were storms that day, and flights were delayed. When I got to Charlotte, I had only a few minutes to reach my connecting flight to DC. As I started rushing to get to the terminal, I began having trouble breathing. This was an asthma attack! Trying not to panic, I searched for airport assistance. I spotted a staff employee, desperately told him what I was trying to do to catch my flight but expressed that I was also having an asthma attack. Breathing was now a struggle! He quickly radioed for medical assistance. They then whisked me onto a transport vehicle and headed toward my terminal. They told me that if my breathing didn't improve, they would immediately take me to the infirmary. Thank God I had that inhaler! I used it immediately and tried to remain calm. The inhaler saved me! I began to breathe better. When we got to my gate of departure, the airport staff members checked me closely and saw that I was okay. I thanked them, boarded the connecting flight, sat back in my seat, and thanked God for what He had done.

I now understood why I had the urging to get the inhaler. I didn't know this attack would occur, but God did, and I was so grateful. When I returned to my job, I told co-workers what had happened to me. I sent an email to other instructors regarding the lesson I had learned, stressing that those having asthma should <u>always</u> be prepared. Their medications must be current and with them. It can be the difference between life and death. I also was able to share the goodness of the Lord and how He had guided me through this ordeal. I was also grateful that He had used Lucille to call and advise me. When I think about the many times, that I know of, that He delivered me through other health challenges, I just feel so loved and blessed.

As adults, we expect to encounter health issues and situations. Yet we are very concerned about our children and what they are going through. God knows all about our worries and concerns. It is so important to talk to Him about whatever it is. With our daughters, we have had and continue to have concerns about them and their future lives without us.

Another health issue I experienced was with Jasmine and Jessica. When they were little girls, I was very concerned about how we would handle their menstrual cycles. Yes, that was a big concern. They weren't like me, as I started my cycle at age 15. My daughters were physically developing quickly, and I was getting worried. I talked to our doctor, who told me that some girls start their cycles as early as eight years old. I thought I would freak out! How in the world would they be able to handle a monthly period? How would they understand it? What would happen if it started at school, and I wasn't with them? What could I do?

The first thing I did was to pray. "Lord," I said, "Please don't let them start early. Please let them be at least 15 years old." I didn't know if the Lord would honor this request or not. I hoped He would. However, He did speak to my mind and said, "start showing them." I have learned to recognize His voice. The Lord is very concise when communicating to me. So, when I had my monthly cycle, I would take them into the bathroom and show them how to manage a period.

Then the Lord led me to write a small book to help them. I was able to get some graphics from a handout that Ivymount had produced. I then used clipart and created simple sentences to explain what to do. Once this personal book was created, the girls and I read it together. I, of course, shared it with Charles and Geoffrey, so that they would know what to do if I was not at home with them. I also made copies of it for the nurses and the girls' teachers at Ivymount. Everyone thought this was a great idea, and we were all on the same page. One important aspect of this process cited in the book was to create a menstrual emergency bag to be with them each day. It consisted of a pouch containing the things they would need: one or two pads, change of panties, and a small plastic bag, if needed, to house soiled underwear. God led me to put these pouches together, place them in their backpacks, and remind the girls of the pouches' purpose. At this point, they couldn't even pronounce the word *menstrual,* nor the word *period.* So, I still prayed that God would not allow their cycles to begin until they were at least teenagers, hoping that by that time, their speech and understanding would be greatly improved.

It was the day of their dental checkup. Both Jasmine and Jessica were 10 years old. It was a Wednesday, which was the abbreviated day of the week at Ivymount. That morning, the "little voice" spoke to my mind, telling me to check to make certain their pouches were inside their backpacks. I checked and each one was there with the appropriate items. I gave them hugs and kisses, and then left for work. Charles, who had received his degree in Ministry, had also become a realtor. So later that day, he called and told me that he had an unexpected real estate appointment. "Can you take the girls to the dentist after they get home from school?" he asked. "Yes," I told him. "I am not teaching today so that won't be a problem." He dropped off Jasmine and Jessica at Dolly's. As previously mentioned, she and her husband Bill were licensed day care providers, lived right down the street, and had also become like family to us. I left work, picked them up, and headed to our dental appointment with Dr. Brown.

As we were getting out of the car at the dental office, "something" spoke to my mind and told me to have the girls take their backpacks with them. When I heard this, I thought that was a good idea, so they could do schoolwork while in the waiting room. Once in the office, after checking in at the front desk, I took the girls to the bathroom. Parents know that this is always advisable, and their children should always "go" before they are sitting in the dentist's chair. When Jessica pulled down her underwear, I noticed that the seat of her little panties was a dark brown color. I said "Jessica, what is this?" She looked at me and I could tell she didn't know. As I continued to examine her, I realized that her cycle had started. But then, I realized, that God had prepared us for this day! Charles couldn't take them, I could, and the Lord had led us through this process. The "little voice" had first reminded me, that morning, to check their backpacks for their pouches. Then the "little voice" had told me to have them carry their backpacks inside the building. Since Jessica's backpack was out in the waiting room, all I had to do was retrieve it, explain to the girls what had happened, and use the contents in the pouch. Having read the book with them, showing them with my own monthly cycle, and being with Jessica when she first started her period, they were fine. I was so grateful that the Lord had arranged that day so that I, their mother, would be with them.

I knew that it was yet another blessing. Although God did *not* stop their cycles from starting, He led and helped us through this health issue. Jasmine's cycle started about six months later. It was on a Saturday, and I was home with her. Yes, God cares about every aspect of our lives. Praise the Lord for yet another blessing!

Chapter 11

LABOR OF LOVE - PART TWO

In 1994 we had survived the labor of love, gained the lives of two special children, and lost the life of one unforgettable woman, Mom. Now, years later, another labor of love developed, the caregiving for Dad. Our journey would become even more challenging and exhausting!

Right after Mom's sudden death, we suggested to Dad that he stay with us. He agreed and temporarily moved in with us. As we were all trying to heal from Mom's devastating departure, it was good having him in our home. Charles and I discussed whether Dad should permanently live with us. But Charles's mother suspected what we were thinking and talked to me about this issue. Mom Gray advised me to let my dad decide what *he* wanted to do. She had experienced the same situation after Charles' dad died. She said, "Your dad is a grown man. He needs time to get adjusted to life without your mom. He needs to determine what he should do." She was a very wise and loving person, so I adhered to her suggestion, which proved to be the correct choice. After a while, Dad returned home and slowly adjusted to life without Mom. He continued to stay busy with church activities and was always available to help our special family as well.

One day after Dad had moved back to his house, I was at home alone with the babies. It had been an uphill battle healing from the pregnancy, the babies' delivery, and Mom's death. I was trying to get my strength back and take care of the girls. I was in the kitchen and heard one of them starting to cry. Rushing to their nursery, I lost consciousness. Upon waking up, I realized I was lying on the floor. Although disoriented, I had not broken any bones. My eyeglasses were bent but amazingly, I felt okay. However, in fear of passing out again, I was afraid to stand up. So, I crawled to our bedroom, was able to reach the phone, called Charles who was at work, and then called Dad. A very dear couple, Aunt Iris and Uncle Alsop who were like family to us, just happened to be visiting Dad. They all quickly came to the house and took care of Jasmine, Jessica and me. Dad was always there to lend a helping hand. He would sometimes take Geoffrey to piano lessons and always supported Geoffrey's extra-curricular activities.

Dad did well for a number of years and even began dating a dear lady, who had also graduated from Hampton Institute. However, we knew he needed help around the house. My plate was quite full working full-time, musically supporting our church fellowship, co-directing the Gospel-Aires, and taking care of three children. We hired a lady to conduct light housekeeping for Dad, who soon told us that he was appearing to have problems remembering certain things. He also had some unfortunate situations occur.

Once, a young man, whom he had hired to cut the grass, stole some of his credit cards. Also, I noticed that he kept copious notes written on yellow legal pads. He would write down things like the bills he paid, the phone calls he had, whom he talked to and what it was about. This information also revealed people taking advantage of him. One entry was from some company that offered to pay Dad to submit blood. That's correct, blood! Trust me, I called them and told them not to call his phone number again! Dad was trying to keep up with paying bills, car maintenance, groceries, and medical appointments. He developed a tremor, which was evidenced in his right hand. He also was involved in two car accidents. Although no one was hurt, he was responsible for causing both of them. We realized that he had a problem. After consulting with his doctor, I took him to be evaluated by a neurologist. The diagnosis was Parkinson's and Alzheimer's.

We now had to make some decisions. First, I had to get control of all his business matters and gain an understanding of how we needed to proceed. I became his power of attorney so that I could make sound decisions for him. Because of his accidents, I knew that it had become too dangerous for him to continue driving a motor vehicle. Technically, if Dad hit someone, with his medical condition, the victims could take legal action against both of us!

Sargent Church members began to tell me how they would spot him driving his car, sitting at an intersection, with the green traffic light in his direction. Then, when the light would turn red, he would "floor" the accelerator, going through the red light. It was time to do the inevitable. When I asked him to give his car keys to me, he became very angry! I will never forget how he threw the keys down on the floor, breaking the key chain. This was a terrible reality for him. He knew that he was losing his independence. To prevent a tragedy, I took the keys and the car. I requested that his doctor write a letter to the Maryland Department of Motor Vehicles, so that he could not obtain another driver's license. Instead, we had it replaced with a Maryland ID card. I also secured other means of transportation for him, including a county taxi service that had reduced rates for senior citizens. Since a few church members lived in his neighborhood, he was easily able to get rides to church. This was indeed a blessing.

Unfortunately, he continued to deteriorate, and we were forced to make a decision. Although his wonderful neighbors did their best to look out for him, they could only do so much. Dad needed assistance, 24 hours a day. Should we get him placed in a nursing home, or should we move him in with us? We thought about it, prayed over it, and decided that we needed to take care of Dad ourselves. Yes, we already had challenges with the girls, but Dad needed us, and we knew that God would get us through. I will always be grateful to my wonderful husband, who was adamant about us taking care of Dad in our home. We did just that.

Several days a week, we took Dad to Crescent Ridge, a senior daycare facility. Eventually, he went there every day, Monday through Friday. The staff was very kind and attentive to Dad. Yes, we had a lot going on. As he continued to lose his cognitive abilities, it was also emotionally difficult for him. One day in 2007, with the girls in the car, I picked up Dad from the facility. I decided to pose some current event questions. I asked the three of them, "Who is the president of the United States?" Silence. Then I asked, "Who is running for president of the United States?" At the time, it was Barack Obama. This was historic and something Dad would have been so happy to articulate. Yet, when asked this question, he could not answer. Silence again. It broke my heart.

Life continued. Dad was prescribed medications to help with both diseases. I learned that although these medications could slow the symptoms of this horrible disease, there was no cure for Alzheimer's. God blessed us to buy some property and we built a house that accommodated Dad's challenges. When we showed him the architectural plans, which remarkably he could still understand, he became so excited. You see, Dad majored in architectural engineering at Hampton Institute, which is now Hampton University. He was very happy and looking forward to living in a wonderful new house.

That day finally came, and we moved into our dream home in June, 2008. The house was fully handicapped accessible, and Dad loved it. It even had an elevator, which allowed Dad to easily access any floor level. However, he needed more care. Since Charles was now a pastor and realtor, his schedule was flexible. One of our friends, Ms. Clover, helped take care of Dad as did one of Charles' sisters, Elsie. We worked hard but it was worth it. Everyone contributed and added joy to Dad's life.

The last two years of his journey with us were very difficult. Regarding Alzheimer's, I could write a separate book about this illness. I learned so much about the disease, all the areas it impacts, and the realization that this disease, because of heredity, could someday come upon me. I learned about organizations that help provide resources to families. I learned how important it is for caregivers to take care of themselves, physically, mentally, emotionally and spiritually. I learned that there are so many families dealing with this disease. I learned the importance of taking breaks from your home, if possible, to simply get away for a short time. I will always be grateful to Evie, one of my choir members, who recommended a wonderful residential home that took care of a few elderly individuals. They usually had a spare bedroom and sometimes I would check Dad in there so that we could all get a break.

This portion of our journey continued to worsen with time. I learned that every time a loved one must be hospitalized or placed into a rehabilitation facility, they "slip" a little; their mental state slightly decreases. This also applies to traumatic events. When Dad's only remaining sibling— his older sister Ruby, who was like a mother to him— died of Alzheimer's in 2009, it was as if Dad fell off of a cliff. He got significantly worse. Not only that, but Mom Gray was also in failing health. Her mind was still sharp, but her body was deteriorating. She was, however, blessed to have seven daughters to take care of her. Her sons, daughters-in-laws, and other family members helped, but her daughters did most of the heavy lifting. She was their labor of love and they did a phenomenal job! There were times when both Dad and Mom Gray were simultaneously hospitalized. During those times, we would often leave one hospital and then proceed to the other.

The last year of Dad's life was really a challenge. He basically couldn't remember anyone or anything. Although he never referred to me as his mother, I could sense that I had become a mother figure to him. I suspected he knew that I was important and that I was responsible for him and his welfare. One time in a hospital emergency room, I was sitting beside his bed, holding his hand. He looked at me and in a rare moment of clarity said, "I know that you are so tired." I assured him that I was okay. But he was correct. I *was* tired, exhausted and mentally drained. He was in and out of hospitals and rehabilitation centers. When he was in rehab facilities, one of my cousins, Sylvia (Aunt Ruby's daughter), would slip into Dad's room and visit with him during very late nighttime hours. We were very blessed to have numerous family, friends, and church members who checked in on him. All these visits helped us monitor how well he was being cared for.

As the diseases progressed, Dad had become a fall risk. I learned about equipment to assist with this problem, including those with alarms that would go off if the person was trying to leave a chair or bed. Dad kept attempting to leave, which often happens with Alzheimer's patients, especially at night. Since he was so unsteady, we were most fearful that he would fall. So, we developed ways to physically restrain him. It was simply awful!

Time lapsed on and his health complications increased. I learned that eventually with Alzheimer's, the body can forget how to swallow and correctly process food. Pneumonia often results. This happened to Dad, so we had to stop giving him regular food. Everything he ate had to be put in a food processor, and liquids had to be thickened. This was a terrible adjustment for him. However, regarding food, there was one humorous moment that occurred. One afternoon, he was sitting at the kitchen table and Elsie was there taking care of him. She left her plate, which contained a few fried chicken wings, to answer her phone. When she returned a few minutes later, she found what was left of her food, chicken bones. Although that could have proven dangerous for Dad, the Lord blessed him, and he did not choke. We laughed about it later, as it was a fond memory of Dad and his love for chicken.

At one point, he had a blood clot and yet again, had to be hospitalized. After that, he went for the last time, to a rehabilitation facility. The medical staff told me that I would have to administer a blood thinner twice daily, using a syringe. I was aghast! I told them that I could not do that; I could not stick anyone with a needle. I told them that I was a teacher and a musician, not a nurse. I'm sure that this was not the first time that they had heard a similar excuse. They told me that I would be fine and instructed me to bring a piece of fruit to the facility, which they would use to teach me how to administer an injection. I kept talking to the Lord. I told him that although I loved my father, I did not understand why this was happening. I was so stressed and heart-broken by all of these events, especially now having to deal with this blood clot situation.

Saying that I learned a lot is an understatement. Ultimately, I learned to give Dad his injections. He was, by now, virtually in a comatose state and when I stuck him with the needle, he never even flinched. After two days of administering his injections, it became, as some would say, "as easy as a piece of cake." I would go into his bedroom prior to going to work, give him his morning injection, and head off to my job. I almost felt like a real nurse!

We obtained hospice care the last couple of months of Dad's life. (*Hospice* is in-home medical care and support for terminally ill people.) Again, this proved to be another learning experience. The hospice personnel were very nice. However, for basic care, one thing I learned was that employees are only with you for a few hours each day. Many people do not realize that fact until their loved one undergoes hospice care. This entire ordeal was very sad, especially to see Dad in this state. I asked God many times, "Why is Dad still here?" His quality of life was completely gone. He could not talk nor communicate. The dad I knew was gone. This was hard on Charles and our family as well. Geoffrey, who now lived in North Carolina, and Larry, who lived in California, had recently visited with us to see Dad. They both knew the end was near. Our choir came and sang to Dad. There were both tears and smiles among all of us.

Then the day came. It was the Friday before Mother's Day, 2010. I was at work and received a phone call from Charles to come home. The hospice team said that Dad was transitioning and that his vitals were diminishing. I rushed home, only to find out that he was still holding on. I put gospel music in the CD player and made sure that Dad was comfortable.

The doorbell rang, Charles answered it, and it was a chaplain from hospice. She was very pretty, dressed in a long, wispy flowing dress. She almost seemed to float into our foyer. When my husband asked what religion she was, she stated that she would be whatever we needed her to be. Charles quickly told her that we appreciated her coming but that we would handle Dad's transition. She smiled and "floated" right back out of the house. It was a little humorous and I will never forget that moment. My dad had been an elder at Sargent Church, and we knew he would want to receive his ascent to heaven from a Christian pastor. Charles would gladly fulfill that role, with love!

A few more hours went by. The hospice nurse told me that Dad's vitals were stationary. She said, "Mrs. Gray, your dad could be in this condition all night long." I prayed for God's guidance and then I sat down beside Dad's bed. I took his hand, held it, and talked to him. I said, "Dad, thanks for being a wonderful father. You know I love you so much. But it is time for you to go. Tell Mom how much I love and miss her. Tell everyone there how much I love and miss them too. But it is time. Thank you for all you have done for me. We will always love you and miss you. I will be fine. I will be okay." Amazingly, within two minutes, the nurse said that his vitals started dropping very quickly. I ran and got Charles. We deliberately made sure Jasmine and Jessica were in another room watching television. Charles closed the room door, and I turned the music volume down low. Holding hands, we all gathered around his bed. Charles began praying and thanking God for Dad's life. After he said Amen, I knelt down to turn up the music volume. When I stood back up, Dad was gone. He was with the Lord.

The hospice team was very touched. One of them was new to the occupation and had never witnessed what she had just seen.

They saw a man, with stable vitals, hear his daughter thank him for his life and love, and essentially give him the comfort in knowing that she would be okay. They saw him being ushered to the Lord in prayer, believing that he had been holding on to receive those final words from me. I learned later that some people refer to this as "giving someone permission to die." I believe that God allowed Dad to get that confirmation from me that I would be okay. He allowed Dad to convey his final act of love and concern for my welfare. Once he got that assurance from me, the Lord took him home.

Unlike Mom's funeral, I remember Dad's well. It was almost like a celebration. What an awesome life! Our father grew up in rural Virginia, fought in one of the first "colored" combat units in World War II, became one of the first African American engineers at the Norfolk Naval Shipyard located in Norfolk, Virginia, and accomplished much during his 89 years of life. He was dedicated to his family, the church, the community and was an inspiration to us all!

While we were caring for Dad, many people, including family members, had voiced their concerns about our labor of love. They articulated that this was a lot to deal with and that we should consider putting him in a nursing home. Yes, it was stressful being a caregiver, especially taking care of two special needs children. I personally encountered much along this journey. In addition to my workload, I also had my share of health-related challenges. There were severe periodic flare-ups with my neck, my lower back, elevated blood pressure occurrences, and more. But I learned so much about medications, dietary complications, buying diaper pads and whatever else was needed to take care of my father. I learned about hospital staff, most of whom were great but a few, not so great. Sometimes when a loved one has Alzheimer's and they cannot adequately communicate, some medical staff may not treat them well. But God always blessed us, as Dad would have a roommate who could tell us what kind of care he was really receiving when we were not physically there. I learned about living wills. I learned a lot about rehabilitation centers. I learned, when he stayed at these facilities, to physically examine Dad to make certain he did not have any bed sores or other issues. Interfacing with medical and administrative staff, I learned patience and diplomacy. We wanted the medical staff to know that we appreciated what they were doing, especially since our loved one was left in their care. I learned that smiling was better than frowning. I prayed a lot.

I had questioned God many times as to why Dad was still alive. I don't remember receiving a response. But obviously, there were things that the Lord wanted me to learn, and therefore, I have been able to advise and hopefully, inspire others. I can understand what caregiving truly is, and that it is indeed a labor of love. You never know what you can do until you must do it. When Dad transitioned, the Lord allowed me to be with him. I learned that despite his comatose state, he could still hear me and understand. I learned that when someone is unconscious or dying, you should talk to them as if they understand because their hearing is one of the last senses to leave. I have shared this with others who have found themselves around the bed of their departing loved one.

I learned the truth of what it says in Philippians 4:13, "I can do all things through Christ who strengthens me." I learned the importance, if possible, of taking care of family. I learned how great it is to have a loving and supportive husband who values taking care of the people who took care of us as children. Most of all, I learned about God's grace. We were also grateful, five months later, to be at the bedside of my dear mother-in-law, Deaconess Pauline V. Gray, as she transitioned to be with the Lord. Our journey had been challenging, to say the least. But our parents blessed us, we blessed them, and through our labor of love, the Lord blessed us all!

Dad's Last Birthday Celebration

Larry and Dad

Chapter 12

AN EXPLOSIVE SITUATION

It was a typical Wednesday, October 6, 2010. We had been through a tough year, as Dad had died in May and Mom Gray in September. In fact, it was a few weeks later after Mom Gray had been funeralized. God had gotten us through, and as most people know, life goes on after the death of loved ones, including parents. Regardless of how we feel, the world just keeps on turning.

On this particular day, Charles received a call from a real estate client, asking him to check on a prospective house. After the call, Charles left home and drove to the house, located about a half hour away. Wednesday was Jasmine and Jessica's short day at Ivymount, but he would have enough time to go, quickly evaluate the status of the house, and return home prior to the girls' arrival from school. Once there, he retrieved the key from the lockbox, a small combination box for the safe storage of a home's key, which allows real estate agents and their clients to access the home when the seller isn't there.

Charles entered the vacant house. He began to check it out, surveying its condition upstairs first, and then walking down the steps to the basement. While visually evaluating the ceiling and the ventilation system, he noticed that the ducts were not quite right. In fact, here is what he later told a WUSA TV news reporter: "I noticed, while looking downstairs into the basement, that the ducts were out of place. When I reached in to adjust the vents, I felt a bag. When I pulled on the bag, two pipe bombs fell into my hands." Lord have mercy!

As he collected himself, he remained calm and proceeded to figure out what to do. First, he had to get away from the bombs. Second, he knew he could not wait for the police to get there because he had to get home before the girls got home from school. He was in a dilemma. God gave him wisdom, and he quickly saw a nearby bathroom with an area in the ceiling where he could hide the bag containing the bombs. He did not want to leave them exposed in the event that another agent would find them and perhaps be killed. Or the bomb maker might return and make the situation even worse. So Charles hid the bag inside a bathroom ceiling tile, secured the house, left, and called the police. He told them what had happened, where he had placed the bombs, and that he would return as soon as he could.

Charles went home and met the girls' school bus. He called the police again, and they told him to return to the property right away. As he drove back, accompanied by Jasmine and Jessica, he could not help thinking that he was in for quite an experience on this day. Afterall, the police always start with the "bird in hand," right?

I had taken leave from work that afternoon and was at the Department of Motor Vehicles to get Dad's vehicle switched over to our names. My cell phone rang and it was Charles, telling me to leave right away. He quickly told me what was going on and that I needed to meet him at the District Heights house, so that I could take care of the girls. He gave me the address and we ended the call. I couldn't believe what was happening. My husband could have been killed! I left the line I was standing in and believe it or not, although he was wearing a baseball cap and sunglasses, I recognized one of our local TV broadcasters. I assumed he was there to take care of his own personal business. I really wanted to tell him what was going on but knew that time was of the essence and that I needed to get to where Charles was with the girls. I virtually ran out of the building to the car and as I drove, I felt disbelief and some degree of shock. This was absolutely crazy!

Once I got to the District Heights street, I immediately saw police and fire department personnel. They had blocked off the area and no one could get close to the house. After parking the car, I quickly spotted Charles, who was being interrogated by police officials, ran to him for a quick hug, and then went to get the girls out of his truck. They were fine, and as we were walking back to our car, we saw some students who were trying to figure out how they were going to walk home. I quickly went over to them, only to discover that they normally walked down the street of the bomb scene and cut over to another street to get to their apartment complex, thereby avoiding a huge and very busy highway. Amidst all the confusion, I volunteered to drive them home, which they gratefully accepted. Although we were all in a state of disbelief regarding the bombs, I did ask them about school, which they eagerly chatted about. A short time later, I dropped them off at their destination and headed back to the bomb scene.

The entire area was inhabited by police, fire EMS (including the county's fire chief), ATF (Alcohol, Tobacco & Firearms) officials, and the FBI. News media from all of our major local affiliates were there as well as news reporters from radio stations. This was a very big deal! Charles was questioned by law enforcement several times, each one taking their turn to see if his story was credible. He could not help but feel that he might be spending the night in jail!

Soon, we watched as a robot entered the house. A short time later, we heard several explosions, and assumed that it had detonated the devices in the back yard of the home. Charles was interviewed by multiple news outlets and later appeared on numerous broadcasts. Here is one of the news reports:

> "A bomb squad was sent to a District Heights, Maryland, home after a real estate agent found what appeared to be two pipe bombs in the basement. The real estate agent went to the house to inspect it Wednesday afternoon. The residents of the two-story red-brick single family home in the 5800 block of

Kentucky Avenue had recently been evicted," P.G. Cty Fire and EMS spokesman Mark Brady said.

"The real estate agent called authorities. The bomb squad was called at about 3:00 p.m. Authorities could not see inside to determine whether or not it was a real bomb or a fake one, so the bomb squad disrupted it to render it safe," News 4's Aaron Gilchrist reported. "A substance inside the device will be taken to a lab to determine if it is explosive," authorities said.

Frightened neighbors were also aired in this news-breaking story. I myself was even interviewed and videotaped by our CBS news affiliate. As evening approached, I took the girls home. My phone was constantly ringing, as people we knew had seen the news reports. During the afternoon, I had called some of our family and friends, and once at home, I found even our house phone "ringing off the hook."

Due to all of this, I knew that I would need to report this to my agency, which I did the next day. I talked to one of our security officials and informed him of what had happened, including the fact that Charles and I were both interviewed by news media outlets. When I told him that in one interview, Charles had said that what "fell into his hands looked like something you would have seen on *MacGyver*," I chuckled and said that maybe he should have made the comparison to something seen on the TV show (at that time), "24." The official quickly replied that Charles was correct. Pipe bombs of that nature would have been on *MacGyver*, not "24," as the explosive devices on "24" were significantly more sophisticated. Anyway, he stated that he was very glad that my husband was not hurt or killed.

More than anything else, we were grateful that the Lord had kept Charles safe. It could have been a very different outcome. We never found out what actually happened and who was responsible for planting the bombs. All we knew was that we were grateful to God for His grace and most of all, for blessing us with His divine protection!

Chapter 13

ALL IN THE FAMILY

Back in the 1970's, there was a very popular sitcom entitled, *All in the Family*. It starred Carroll O'Connor (Archie), Jean Stapleton (Edith), Sally Struthers (Gloria), and Rob Reiner (Michael aka "Meat Head"). The show revolved around the life of a white, working-class man and his family. It tackled a lot of issues, such as racism, homosexuality, rape, religion, miscarriages, and numerous other controversial subjects. Many of us who watched the show can recount various episodes, and I'm sure you are wondering how this sitcom could possibly be relevant to Jasmine and Jessica. All I can say is, "Only God!"

By the time the girls were about 15 years old, for short periods of time, we would leave them home alone. Charles and I knew that they needed to become independent and responsible. They both had sweet personalities and were naïve to the evils of our present world. Jasmine and Jessica seemed "wired" to be happy and joyful, so we began to better prepare them for dangerous situations. Accordingly, we instructed them that while we were gone and they were home alone, they were never to open the door to anyone or let anyone come into the house. We trusted them and assumed that they were obeying our instructions.

One day, Charles and I went out to run some errands and upon returning home, noticed a UPS box sitting in our foyer. We immediately called Jasmine and, when she came downstairs, asked her how the box got into the foyer. She replied that she had let the man in and that he put the box on the foyer floor. We were immediately upset; not only had she disobeyed us, but she had let a total stranger enter our home without us being on the premises. So now we had to sit down and again talk to both her and Jessica. We told them that even though someone is wearing a uniform, they were still not to open the door to that person or anyone else. We told them that a bad person could pretend to be a good person and hurt them. We explained again the dangers of letting a stranger into our house, and that they could be attacked, raped, or even killed.

After our talk, I went into the family room, turned on the television and started scrolling through the channels. To my surprise, I saw that *All in the Family* was coming on, which I hadn't seen in years. It was rare that this show was being aired, so I eagerly began watching it. I immediately realized that this episode was the one about rape. My mouth dropped in disbelief.

I remembered it well. Edith, Archie's wife, was almost raped by a very nicely dressed young man who came to her door pretending to be a salesman. She allowed him to come into their home, and once he realized that she was alone, he tried to rape her. This episode was a perfect example for Jasmine and Jessica to watch. Since I immediately remembered the plot, I quickly got them to sit with me and watch it, as I explained the ongoing drama. With Jasmine and Jessica being visual learners, this was an ideal learning experience for them. They saw the young man, who had pulled out a knife, threaten Edith. They saw him chasing her around the house and the panicked expression on her face. It amazingly illustrated what Charles and I had just told them about not letting anyone come into our home. They were fully engaged in the drama taking place on the television screen and by the end of the program, seemed to understand the possible danger that we had communicated to them. In other words, they got it!

Afterwards, Charles and I talked about God's goodness and how this was indeed a blessing. Out of all the 200 or more episodes of *All in the Family,* this was the one that came on, right when it was needed to provide a visual and dramatic presentation for our daughters to see. Not only was the program on the same day, but it also occurred within minutes of us speaking to the girls on the program's subject matter. Incredible!

One of the aspects of this journey that I have learned is that God cares about *all* our cares, no matter how big, no matter how small!

Chapter 14

A DIVINE GRADUATION TIME

What a wonderful time in our lives! Jasmine and Jessica were graduating from Ivymount's high school program. Although they did not receive a high school diploma, they did receive a certificate. Also, their educational programming was to continue. They would enter Ivymount's post-high school program, which would concentrate on employment development. Again, this was paid for by our county. We never paid a dime. Glory be to God!

We were so happy for our girls. It had been a long road, and trust me, we had had our share of bumps along the way, especially regarding their transportation. Sometimes their bus rides took two hours and sometimes longer, especially if they encountered severe traffic delays. Also, their buses were not air-conditioned. During the summers, this was indeed uncomfortable, as some days were well into the upper nineties (Fahrenheit) with high levels of humidity. We tried to get them transferred to a bus with air-conditioning, especially since Jessica had asthmatic symptoms early in her youth. Unfortunately, we were unable to get this accomplished. Also, due to their long commutes, especially in the afternoon, they were unable to properly hydrate during the day. Fluids were curtailed as their school buses did not have rest rooms. Because Jessica had accidentally wet herself a couple of times during extremely long commutes, she was even put on a medication that helped improve her bladder control. Despite these "bumps," the Lord protected the girls from bus accidents and breakdowns.

Ivymount provided high-quality instruction through technology, small classes with individualized instruction, and extensive speech therapy. Although the girls still had a significant speech disability and

109

were intellectually challenged, they continued to develop. They excelled in sports such as bowling, and even now, really "shine" in the area of singing and dancing. Because they were so visual, if you showed them how to do something, they could do it. Jasmine and Jessica had watched Disney's High School Musical video so many times, that they basically knew every dance routine. When Ivymount performed this musical, Jasmine and Jessica were selected as the lead dancers. Several teachers referred to them as "the stars of the show" and the girls gave a dynamic performance! Ivymount is a special school filled with dedication, teamwork, and love.

On a wonderful Friday in June 2012, family, friends and church members were at Ivymount to witness the girls' graduation program. The next day, we had a big celebration party at our home, and blessings had already begun to manifest themselves. I had picked two of the girls' favorite colors, pink and purple, as the color scheme. Lisa, one of my prayer partners from work, gave me balloons and a small gift for each of them. Although I had not told her the color scheme, the balloon gift packages were pink and purple! I was able to include her balloons with the other room decorations.

We were all so excited! I was happy but also nostalgic as so many memories flooded my mind. I remembered how Mom was looking forward to being a grandmother again, this time with two granddaughters. I thought of Dad and Mom Gray, including so many challenges we had experienced. But I snapped out of my memories to focus on myself and my immediate need: clothing! Jasmine and Jessica were wearing their favorite light purple skirts with white tops. I, on the other hand, had nothing to wear. As I had physically put on a few pounds, everything I tried on was too small. I would have loved to wear something that consisted of the color scheme, but I had not prepared an outfit for the occasion. Despite my weight gain, I had the audacity to want Charles' brother's wife Carolyn to bring her scrumptious red velvet cake. When I learned that Carolyn and some of Charles' sisters had already planned to bring food, I decided not to ask Carolyn to bake a cake for us after all. There would be plenty of deserts.

I still did not know what I was going to wear. Soon, Dolly came over early to help with the celebration. She shoved a bag into my hands and told me to try it on. I looked in the bag and it was a dress. I couldn't believe it. Only God knew I needed something to wear. I asked her why she did this. She told me that "something" kept urging her to bring me this dress from her closet, which she had never worn. She fought against the urging, got the other items she was bringing with her, and got in her car to leave from her house to ours. The urging was so strong that she went back into the house and retrieved the dress for me. I told her that I needed a dress, as I had nothing to wear. The dress was a long, flowing, sleeveless summer dress, very attractive and appropriate for the occasion. As I stood there in our bedroom, looking at myself in the mirror, I felt tears well up in my eyes. My new pink, purple, and white dress fit perfectly. It was the right color and size. What a gift from God!

The incredible day progressed. Jasmine and Jessica's friends from Ivymount, some of whom had graduated along with the girls, and their parents were there. One of them, Andale, had a beautiful baritone voice and often would sing solos at the Ivymount musical programs. We asked him to sing and he sang acapella (no accompaniment), one of his favorite songs, "What A Wonderful World". While he sang, he took Jessica by the hand and danced with her. Among the adults present, I suspect there were no dry eyes in the room. To say that the Lord blessed was an understatement. Not only did the girls and everyone there have a fantastic time, but God also blessed me in only ways that He could have done. Remember Dolly provided my dress. To my surprise, Carolyn brought a red velvet cake. She told me that she was not going to make one, but "something" kept urging her to do so. She had made the cake that morning. I felt that God was showing me His love and was blessing me for all I had done to bless my children. I was so humbled. We ate, the young people danced, the girls opened their gifts, and we simply had a glorious time.

Later that evening, after almost everyone had gone home, Charles and I sat at the kitchen table, discussing our wonderful day. Joyce, one of Charles' sisters, was still there with us. I turned my head and noticed a large gift bag that we had overlooked. It was from Charles' brother, Bernard, and Carolyn. I brought it over to the table and pulled out one of two somewhat heavy grey-colored boxes. I carefully opened one of them, and we saw that it was a beautiful water globe containing a gorgeous round silver snowflake, studded with diamond-looking stones. As I shook it, silver glitters flew around inside. "Something" told me to turn it upside down and in doing so, I spotted a musical switch. I wound it and we started listening to the little song it played. When I recognized it, I was stunned! I looked at Joyce in amazement. It was the song "What A Wonderful World"! It was as if the Lord had orchestrated everything and "dotted the end of the sentence" of a perfect day, with the same song Andale had sung. Out of all the songs in the world, this was the one that was now playing.

I called Carolyn the next day to tell her about the water globes and was even more amazed. She said that they had already given Jasmine and Jessica gift cards, which was fine. But before they left from their home that day, "something" urged her to retrieve these water globes, which she had purchased months earlier. She had not acquired them for anyone in particular and did not know what song they played. She started to ignore the urging, but was obedient, simply placed them in a gift bag, unwrapped, and brought them with her.

The Lord wasn't finished. When I went to work on Monday, I stopped by the Duncan Donuts stand, located in my building. As I was preparing to pay for my coffee and food, the cashier told me not to. I responded, "Why not?" She said that someone had paid for it. There had been no one in the line I knew and now there was no one in front of me. This had never happened to me. Another blessing!

Often parents, especially those with special needs children, question themselves as to whether they are doing everything they can to promote their children's development. I felt that the Lord was personally blessing me, letting me know that I, as a mom, was doing fine. I will always believe that He reminded me, through the actions of others, just how much he loves me. I thank Him for His blessings and most of all His love!

**Graduation Prom
Jasmine and Jessica**

Post-High School Graduation Day
Jasmine, Charles & Jessica

Chapter 15

POST-HIGH SCHOOL PROTECTION

After graduating from the Ivymount School, Jasmine and Jessica entered Ivymount's four-year post-high school program. Those years not only furthered their education, but also nurtured independent living skills. For example, they learned basic cooking procedures and gained some familiarization with the metro transportation system, to include the trains. Jasmine and Jessica gained "real work" experience at outlets, such as Old Navy, libraries, CVS drugstore, and other businesses.

For the last year of post-high school, they were accepted into a program entitled, "Project Search," which allowed them to become interns at the Smithsonian Museum in Washington DC. This was quite an adjustment. They went from riding the little yellow school bus to riding Metro Access buses. Metro Access, which is a component of the Washington Metropolitan Area Transit Authority (WMATA), services clients with disabilities. They received some travel training, including from WMATA, and since I had retired in early 2014, I was free to train them as well. With my assistance, they learned how to use the commuter bus from our neighborhood bus stop and then travel to and from a bus stop a couple of blocks from the Smithsonian. After their training, we prayed that the Lord would keep our children safe.

In addition to some classroom instruction, most of the girls' hours were spent at their work sites. During the program, three rotations were to occur. Both Jasmine and Jessica had some difficulties with their first placement. Jessica's teachers realized that Jessica needed more than one task to do on a daily basis.

115

Accommodations had to be made for her. Once that was done, she was much more productive and successful. In her first rotation, Jasmine also had some challenges.

Some of the employees who interfaced with Jasmine and Jessica had never worked closely with disabled youth. Other Project Search youth encountered similar challenges. This happens in "real life." It is indeed a learning experience for everyone.

Fortunately, Jasmine's second rotation was great. Her supervisor, Mr. Upchurch, had never closely worked with someone like Jasmine, but he did a fantastic job. In fact, Jasmine performed so well that he requested that she remain and stay there for the third rotation. We were so proud of her! Mr. Upchurch gave her an excellent evaluation and said that if they had been hiring, he would have recommended her. She was a great office worker and enjoyed working at the Portrait Gallery.

The Lord continued to keep the girls safe. When Jasmine started her second rotation, her position required her to walk from the Smithsonian to catch a metro train. Once at the Metro Center station, she then would have to walk two blocks to get to her job. One of her teachers started training her on how to use the metro trains. Unfortunately, on the second day of training, her teacher was sick and did not report to work. She called me and said she would try to get Jasmine on a commuter bus to the gallery. When that didn't materialize, she called Jasmine and asked if she could take the metro train by herself. Jasmine said "yes" and did so. Without my knowledge, Jasmine walked from her building, caught the metro train, got off at the correct stop, and walked to the Portrait Gallery. Although I didn't know what was going on, I tried calling Jasmine. I could not reach her for a while and became very upset. I was even more upset when I called her teacher and finally learned that Jasmine had made the trip alone. Thank God for protection! On the way to the gallery, she travelled alone. On the way back, a fellow student from the building was with her. Unfortunately, the train did not stop at their station. Jasmine called me and was, of course, upset. I told her to get help from a station employee, and the employee helped them get back to their correct station. Once again, I was grateful to God for her protection, and we were very proud of her!

Not only did the Lord protect Jasmine and Jessica, but He also protected their fellow Ivymount students. Those young people were almost like sisters and brothers. Most of them had known each other since they were young children at this special school. One day, at the Smithsonian building that housed their classroom, one of their friends left his wallet on a Smithsonian commuter bus. He was very upset, left his classroom, and headed out of the building on an unknown pursuit to find it. Again, another blessing occurred. I was there that day, taking the metro, learning more travel information to help train our daughters. When I went to their building and approached the front door, he rushed out. I stopped him and asked him where he was going. He said he had left his wallet on a commuter bus. I took him back inside. It was only a miracle that God had placed me there at that very time. He was very upset, and he would not have known what to do or where to go to find his wallet. I called his mom, and she was able to assure him that we had everything under control. Fortunately, the commuter bus driver located us and returned his wallet. Later, his mom and I reminded him, as well as Jasmine and Jessica, that if something happens, they should call us and never leave the safety of their building.

I thanked God that He had used me to prevent a possible tragedy and to remind this wonderful young man how much God loved him. We were so grateful that the Lord had placed me there at the right place, at the right time. It reminded us how the Lord was blessing our children and keeping them safe from harm!

Chapter 16

THE GIFT

He did it again! Yes, God supernaturally blessed us, including our church fellowship, *Spirit of Truth Christian Church*, founded by my dear husband, Pastor Gray. One of our responsibilities is that of conducting the youth message. We traditionally have our children/youth come up to the front of the church to receive a biblical lesson. Oftentimes, we briefly discuss a topic or current event and relate it to God's word. On July 21, 2019, it was my turn to deliver the lesson. Here is what I shared with our youth, my message entitled, "The Gift":

> Last Sunday, Ms. Angie talked to you about the Holy Spirit....and I want all of you to know about something that just happened that we know was led by the Holy Spirit, right before Father's Day. In a previous lesson, I showed you a picture of my cousin George Morris, who works at the University of Virginia (UVA). Remember I told you that he is the Federation of Christian Athletes representative and mentors the men's football and basketball teams? Well, his wife, Mabel, was told by doctors, which is called a diagnosis, that she is in the beginning stage of cancer. We have been praying for her. Well, I ordered Father's Day gifts online this year. Normally, I don't send Father's Day gifts to my cousins, but this year, the Holy Spirit led me to send gifts to two of them. Georges' gift was the second one I ordered. I texted Mabel that George would receive something from us and asked that she look out for it and put it away until Sunday, which was Father's Day.

> Friday, late afternoon, George called me. He told me that he had received our gift. I could hear some excited emotion in his voice. I told him that I was hoping that Mabel would have intercepted it, but he said she was, because of her health situation, understandably asleep when he returned home. He

119

then told me about the fact that he had ministered to a young man earlier that day. He had been led, by the Holy Spirit, to give the young man his bracelet that he normally wore every day. It was black leather, stainless steel, and a scripture was engraved on the stainless-steel portion of it.

When George came home, he saw that a box was addressed to him, opened it, and found the gift from us, which was a bracelet made of black leather, stainless steel, and the following scripture: "With God all things are possible." He was really amazed, as was I. It was such a reminder of how God knows everything. Pastor Gray reminds us that God is *never* surprised by anything. So George and I verbally summarized together, what God had done: The Holy Spirit led me to send George a gift. Out of all the items I could have chosen, I was led to send him this bracelet. George had been led to give *his* bracelet to the young man. George physically received our gift, which replaced the one he gave away on the same day. Finally, his new bracelet also exhibited scripture that was a powerful reminder of God's power. Both he and I laughed for several minutes. We talked about how incredible this was, and how God knows everything we do. Of course He does! Most of all, the Lord loves us so much that He takes the time to do these wonderful things.

So as Pastor Gray has been preaching about, "We sow and we plant," so that people can know the love and power that they can have through Christ Jesus. No other religion has this, which is the gift of the Holy Spirit inside of us. We have the Father, Son, and Holy Spirit. So trust Him, obey His word, believe in Him, and He will let you know that He is real!

That concluded my youth message. The following Sunday should have been Minister Harley's Sunday to deliver the youth message. However, he was preaching that day, his first message as a minister of our congregation. Ms. Angie was in charge of the reception planned for the conclusion of the service, so she had enough responsibility. I asked Charles (Pastor Gray) to do the youth message, but he declined. This was surprising, as he had never before turned me down for virtually anything. So, as one of the three youth message leaders, it was left up to me.

I now had to search for a topic and begin my research. On the Friday night leading up to that Sunday, I searched the Internet. Jasmine (my shadow child) sat at my desk with me. I said to her, "How about searching for July 28," which was the day of the service, to see if there were any interesting events that I could use for the message. She agreed. One possibility was that on July 28, 1945, a plane crashed into the Empire State Building. Thick fog had caused the B-25 bomber to crash into it. I contemplated writing the lesson about a woman, who survived a plunge of 75 stories, over 1,000 feet, in a lift within the building. It was a miracle that she survived the aftermath of the crash. Also, when the elevator safety cable broke, she fell down many floors. She broke her back and endured multiple surgeries. Although this was fascinating, I did not feel compelled to use this account. Still connected to the date, I decided to continue my research in another area.

I discovered that James Weldon Johnson (June 17, 1871– June 26, 1938), an exceptional African American writer and civil rights activist, had initiated a historic event. In 1916, Johnson started working as a field secretary and organizer for the National Association for the Advancement of Colored People (NAACP), which had been founded in 1910. In this role, he engaged the NAACP in mass demonstrations. On July 28, 1917, he organized a silent protest parade of more than 10,000 African Americans down New York City's Fifth Avenue to protest the still-frequent lynchings of blacks in the South. I reviewed his poetry. It was obvious that he believed in the Lord. Jasmine liked the poem "The Creation" even more than the one we read entitled "The Prodigal Son." Then I looked at his lyrics of "Lift Ev'ry Voice and Sing." Due to our choir at Hampton Institute (Hampton University now) frequently singing Dr. Roland Carter's beautiful arrangement of "Lift Ev'ry Voice," I knew the lyrics by heart. But for some reason, my spirit wasn't settled on this topic for my youth message. It was very late at night now, so I logged off my computer and went to bed.

Saturday morning, the "little voice" told me to tell the youth
about supernatural occurrences, directed by the Holy Spirit. The
voice told me to tell them the story about the day of Jasmine and
Jessica's graduation celebration from Ivymount...including the
water globes. Since I had just recently delivered the message
entitled "The Gift," I entitled this lesson "The Gift, Part 2." I
questioned myself, "Should I take one of the water globes to
show during the lesson?" The last thing I wanted was to
accidentally drop and break it. Perhaps I should simply take a
picture of it. No, the "little voice" told me to take it, so I carefully
packed one of the globes to carry to the service the next day.

Charles asked me to have a concise youth message, not too
lengthy, so that Minister Harley would have plenty of time to
preach his sermon. I read aloud the youth message and timed
it. It was two minutes long, but I knew that the awesome account
of God's blessings on that day would take a little longer to
present. Here is how the message was to begin:

> Last Sunday's message was entitled "The Gift." This message is
> "The Gift Part 2," a reminder of the greatest gift of all, which is
> the gift of God's love, Jesus Christ, and the Holy Spirit. This
> message has another true story.

In summarizing the message, I would convey to the youth about
the day of Jasmine and Jessica's graduation celebration. I would
tell them how I needed something to wear, and how our friend
Dolly brought me just the right dress. I would share with them
how I wanted the girls' Aunt Carolyn to bring her famous red
velvet cake. I would recount the wonder of Andale's song, the
water globes, and the acts of love I received that day through the
urging of the Holy Spirit. I would recite the scripture to them
from Matthew 10:20, "For it is not ye that speak, but the Spirit
of your Father which speaketh in you"....telling them that only
God could have done all of this, which was a reminder of His
power and love! I would conclude with, "His spirit will lead us
and help us, if we love, believe in Him, trust Him and obey.
Praise God!"

Sunday morning came and I had concerns about the length of the youth message. I decided to postpone this lesson for another time. While Jasmine and Jessica fixed breakfast (yes, they can cook a complete breakfast of bacon, eggs, and pancakes!), I again searched the Internet, this time spotting a reference to Evil Knievel. He had later given his life to Christ, so I started to quickly create a lesson on him. But the "little voice" said, "No, do the gift message." The "little voice" again urged me take one of the water globes as a "visual" and obediently, I did. Still, I was so concerned about the message's length of time that I even told the girls that I may have to skip it and if so, we would need to be flexible. One characteristic of special needs individuals is that if something is planned to occur, they expect it to happen. Period. Once I explained that I might skip the youth message because of time constraints, they understood.

Sunday service had just begun and to my shock, Carolyn and Bernard came into the room to join our worship service. They sat in a front row. We did not know that they were coming to visit our church on that Sunday. They live quite a distance away in Northern Virginia. They didn't know about the content of my youth message. We also found out after the service that the Lord had told Carolyn that they needed to come to our church service. Why was this significant? Remember, Carolyn was one of the people who blessed me at the celebration with the red velvet cake. During the youth message, I added that as an impromptu fact, of which she, from her seat, chimed in telling the young people, "That's right. I had not planned to bake a cake that morning, but the Lord told me to do it." After the service, when I shared how the Lord had instructed me to create this lesson, as opposed to other subjects, and that He had guided Carolyn and Bernard to the service, everyone was speechless. Remember, Carolyn and Bernard had given the girls the water globes, containing the song, "What A Wonderful World." They were a key component of the youth lesson, yet they had no idea that they would be an integral part of it. It was as if God had dotted the end of the sentence yet again. Carolyn and Bernard were gift givers, but the Lord had truly been the real gift giver. He blessed us yet again by guiding the youth message, its creation, and execution, which included Carolyn and Bernard. He taught our youth and everyone else in our church service, how important it is to listen to that "small voice," which is the Holy Spirit within us. We were so blessed by this gift of love and had no idea how His voice, the following year, would save my life!

Chapter 17

A PANDEMIC

Charles Dickens penned these words at the beginning of *A Tale of Two Cities*, which were so indicative of what began in 2020:

> It was the best of times, it was the worst of times, it was the age of wisdom, it was the age of foolishness, it was the epoch of belief, it was the epoch of incredulity, it was the season of Light, it was the season of Darkness, it was the spring of hope, it was the winter of despair, we had everything before us, we had nothing before us, we were all going direct to Heaven, we were all going direct the other way. [The words "epoch of incredulity" simply mean a memorable event of disbelief.]

When I was a high school student, as an English assignment, I had to read this epic novel. I struggled to like it. It seemed so boring. I just could not get into it. "How can I read this awful book?" I asked my mom. With her infamous wisdom, she replied, as best as I can remember, "Put the book down, clear your mind, and start reading it again from the beginning." I took her advice and it worked. I became so involved in the plot that I could barely put it down. It captivated me. And now years later, I reflect on that eloquent beginning line that Mr. Dickens wrote, marveling at its uncanny connection to 2020. Unlike the book, I wanted to put 2020 down, forever. I was not captivated. I was held captive; we all were, in one of the most traumatic years of our lives.

Everyone in our world has a story to tell about the worse pandemic of our lifetime. You may call it *Covid-19* or the *Coronavirus*. The name doesn't matter. It affected every aspect of our beings. Everyone has feelings and opinions surrounding

125

this devastating virus. Many of us knew people who died. We could not visit those who were sick. We could not attend most funerals or church services. Children could not go to school. You could not be physically seen by your doctor or dentist. We all have a story and whether you believe in God or not, we all have a testimony.

Isn't it amazing how we celebrated New Year's Eve, December 31, 2019? Do you remember what you did on that night? Some went out to various celebrations and parties, some stayed at home, and some went to church services. Our family went to our church and had a wonderful time. Prior to our service, we had dinner there. It was delicious! Most of it was "soul food," which included pig feet and black-eyed peas, just to name a couple of items. Then we had an awesome combined worship service with Household of Faith Ministries. Shortly after midnight, we boxed up the remaining food and headed for home.

But this is what is interesting. Each year when we gather in worship and prayer, I always wonder what is going to transpire in the next year. I'm sure everyone else does as well. I always feel thankful and blessed, but secretly, a little apprehensive about what lies ahead. This New Year's Eve, I asked the Lord to help me grow in Him and to reach a higher level of spirituality. Little did I know that this would be a year that we would never forget, and growth in Him would be an understatement.

January was somewhat ordinary, yet we were attending more funerals than we had in previous months. Then the helicopter crash killing Kobe Bryant, his daughter, and all those aboard rocked our nation. Even though many of us had never met Kobe, we were all grieved. That grief and the additional grief we experienced from the deaths of others continued into February.

But God was gracious. He had also blessed us with another year of marriage. On February 5th, Charles and I celebrated our 26th wedding anniversary. We left town for Ocean City, Maryland, and stayed there for several days. During the winter months, the hotel rates are less expensive, and we had a great time. Aunt Woncey stayed with Jasmine and Jessica. She had stayed with them on previous occasions and was very familiar with their daily routines. Charles and I ate at tasty restaurants, and we even went to the movies, which was a rare activity for us. Returning from our little getaway, we dove back into our very full schedules, not anticipating that our journey would take us into an existence that our present world had never experienced.

What a busy time! In a couple of months, April 2020 was going to be jammed packed. The first weekend included Palm Sunday. The Sargent Gospel-Aires were celebrating its 39th choir anniversary on that Saturday. Both Marilyn, our other choir director, and I had been diligently learning music and teaching the choir their vocal parts. Jasmine and Jessica were also choir members and eagerly looking forward to our upcoming concert. Charles, who would be playing keyboards as well, was also practicing for the concert, as were Dennis (our drummer) and the other musicians scheduled to accompany us. The second Sunday was Easter weekend, again a very busy time for us church folks. The third weekend was the Hampton Alumni Choir Anniversary concert, taking place on the campus of Hampton University, my Alma Mater. That concert was to be conducted by the illustrious Dr. Roland M. Carter. It was also my birthday weekend. I was so looking forward to singing with the other alumni members and having a glorious time.

The fourth weekend and the days preceding it, would also be very busy. The Northern Virginia Ministers' Wives and Widows organization, of which I am a member, was to host the Virginia State convention of these wonderful ladies. For the past two years, our chapter had been diligently preparing for this event. Aunt Woncey would also be attending and would be my room-mate at the hotel where all the events were scheduled to take place. So much would be going on that month. I vividly remembered that I prayed and asked the Lord, "Please help get me through April. I need your strength." Little did I know that *all* of these events would soon be cancelled!

By February, we began hearing more about this virus and in March, we started buying essentials. I even began purchasing masks. As the month of March proceeded, we kept seeing news reports about this Covid-19 virus and its impact on other countries. Soon, our focus dramatically changed, as we realized that the virus was here in our country and quickly spreading. People were sickened and deaths resulted. President Trump and his team had determined that our country would have to temporarily shut down. Never had we experienced anything like this. On the fourth Sunday of March, we began doing something that we had never done before, which was worshipping God online. Our county and state were in total lockdown mode. From his office in our home, my husband began broadcasting our Spirit of Truth Christian Church (SOTCC) worship services. Since I am the church's musician, I supplied the music, including vocal solos. Due to the lockdown, we no longer had our praise dancers and youth choir to contribute to our services. There was no longer participation with the Gospel-Aires, as again, our churches were closed. Our lives, as well as everyone else's, were no longer the same. We thought that this would only last a few weeks. How wrong we were!

Our dilemma now was to figure out what Jasmine and Jessica should do. They were still working at this point. Soon, it was determined that they were considered "essential employees." Jasmine is a food services worker at Ft. Meyer, an army base in Arlington, Virginia. Jessica is a food services worker at the Marine Barracks in Southeast Washington, DC. Declaring their "essential status," the Army supplied Jasmine with a letter and the Marines supplied Jessica with a similar letter. We made copies that we kept in both vehicles so that if stopped by the authorities, we had a legitimate reason to be out on the road, providing transportation for our daughters.

We now knew that this disease was very contagious and deadlier for older people, especially those with other health issues, such as high blood pressure. Charles and I both fell into this category. Although masks had not yet been required, I directed both girls to wear them. One day when I questioned Jasmine regarding her ride returning home, she told me that a man on the Metro Access bus was coughing. Now I knew that it was time to end the girls' reliance on public transportation. We began taking both Jasmine and Jessica to and from work. That meant that on Mondays, Wednesdays, and Fridays, Charles or I had to leave each morning at 5:45 a.m. Due to a Covid scheduling change, which actually helped, Jasmine no longer worked on Thursdays. On Tuesdays and Thursdays, we transported Jessica to work. Fortunately, those two days began a little later in the morning, so we didn't have to get up at the crack of dawn.

For a few days, I stopped the girls from reporting to their jobs because by now, we knew that they could transport Covid germs into our house. I needed some time to process this reality, to think, and most of all, to pray. Charles and I discussed the situation and we decided to allow our daughters to continue to work. We prayed and asked God to keep us all safe.

Their workplace environments had incorporated uniform mask wearing, daily temperature checks, and PPE's (personal protective equipment) to wear. This made me feel more secure in our decision to allow them to work. I also established our own regiment. They had to completely cover their hair with a machine-washable scarf-like cap. Once they arrived back home, they had to leave their shoes in the garage, wash their hands, immediately remove all their clothing, take showers, and wipe areas inside the house that they had touched. This was our "new normal."

JASMINE

In January 2020, Jasmine had some sort of strange virus. Due to its nature, I took her to urgent care, where they suggested I take her to the nearest hospital emergency room (ER). On the TV monitor in the hospital waiting room, I noticed a news story, showing people wearing masks in China. As there were many sick people in the ER, we waited for hours. Finally, Jasmine was seen, tests were run, and it was determined that she had some type of virus. We left the hospital around 12:30 a.m., returned home, and went to bed. The doctor said that Jasmine should rest, drink fluids, and that she would be fine. In retrospect, did she have Covid? I don't know and may never know. I *do* know that this virus was strange because her diarrhea was a bright red in color, which we had never seen before. Fortunately, none of us caught whatever she had. She was fine in a few days and returned to work.

Unfortunately, while on her way to work on the morning of February 12, 2020, Jasmine was in a Metro Access bus accident. A dump truck forced their bus into a construction barrier, and unfortunately, never stopped. She called us and we could hear that she was crying. We immediately left home to meet her. Once there, the Metro Access driver said that as he tried to maintain control, the bus jerked back and forth. He then pulled off at the next exit. Jasmine was very upset and began complaining about her lower back hurting. We knew that she needed immediate medical attention. At our doctor's office, it was determined that she had a lower back sprain and was placed on medications.

Over the course of the next nine months, Jasmine would miss time from work, be placed on various pain medications, wear a back brace to her job, and undergo many weeks of physical therapy. Due to the Covid-19 lockdown, it took some time before she was able to see an orthopedic doctor and obtain additional tests. Finally, an MRI showed a slight bulging of two disks in her lower back, which explained why she was still experiencing pain. Fortunately, she did not have any pain or tingling in either of her legs. We were grateful, as it could have been so much worse.

Emotionally, Jasmine seemed well. A couple of times, she *did* burst out crying. I would hug her and ask her what was wrong. She would say, "Covid, Mommy. People are dying." I would console her and tell her that it was good for her to cry. On one of these occasions, I happened to call my brother Larry, who spoke with her in a very consoling manner. He told her that tears were a good thing, and that it was good for her to let it out. Otherwise, she had handled everything going on as well as could be expected. Little did I know that she would soon begin to suffer and take on characteristics she had never before experienced.

JESSICA

In March, Jessica began complaining of headaches and said that her hair was too tight. A couple of months earlier, Jasmine, Jessica and I had received hair weaves. Although Jasmine and I were fine, Jessica continued to complain about her head hurting. Every day her headaches continued. Finally, Charles, using our own blood pressure machine, decided to check her blood pressure and it was indeed elevated. We assumed that this was the cause of her headaches. Since it was elevated again the following day, which was the third Sunday in March, I did not go to church service that day and stayed home with her. Our church fellowship was scheduled to meet later that afternoon and evangelize out in the community. When Jessica's blood pressure continued to escalate, I called my Aunt Barbara in Portsmouth, Virginia. She is a retired nurse and advised me to take Jessica to the emergency room. I told Charles to please proceed with the church's plans and I would get Jessica taken care of. I didn't really want to go to the hospital, as we knew that

Covid-19 was beginning to impact our community. To my surprise, very few people were in the ER. I thought to myself, "Wow, people are scared to come to the hospital unless it is a matter of life or death." The medical staff took Jessica's vitals. Her blood pressure was somewhat elevated. After monitoring her, it continued to improve. But since her numbers were still a little elevated, they instructed me to monitor her, keep her home from her job to rest on the following day, and follow up with our doctor.

Our hair weaves were taken out a couple of days later and to our dismay, Jessica's hair net, underneath the weave, had cut into her scalp. Unknown to us, the hair net must have been defective. As we saw the matted blood and condition of her head, we were stunned. I almost cried. That was the reason for the headaches and elevated blood pressure. After washing her hair, our hair stylist expertly cleaned the area and administered first aid. I then scheduled an appointment with the doctor a couple of days later, who verified that, thankfully, Jessica's head wound was not infected. After that, we continued to treat it and as time progressed, it completely healed. No more headaches, and no more elevated blood pressure. Another reminder of having "special" children: Jessica could not effectively communicate what she was feeling. This is a situation that we as parents experience as they frequently do not communicate like we do. So often, we have to almost guess what is wrong with our children. Thank God that the Holy spirit also helps us with these challenges.

The month of April drastically changed, and all our plans were now cancelled. We were supposed to have gone on a family cruise in May. We had been blessed to go on two cruises in past years, and Aunt Woncey had gone with us. Jessica was now devastated! No one in the family dreamed more of going on a cruise than Jessica, and now the trip she had been excited about for months was no longer a reality. She, as well as her sister, were now living and working in a strange scary new world. The military personnel at their jobs no longer came into the dining halls to sit down to eat. All food acquisitions were now in the form of carryout. Jessica's kitchen responsibilities were the same. However, Jasmine's food service duties had changed, and she was now performing more cleaning than before. As stated previously, they were now wearing PPE's and having daily temperature checks. They were also hearing a host of frightening information and unfortunately, the television screens at their jobs often displayed news coverage.

One day in early March 2020, Jessica began having stomach cramps. This and a couple of other GI (gastrointestinal) symptoms periodically lasted for months. Due to the pandemic and the shutdown, Jessica could not see our primary care physician. I had to take her to urgent care twice, especially to make certain that she did not have Covid. Since GI symptoms were now associated with the virus, she needed to be tested. Thank God, she tested negative each time! However, the stomach cramping continued, and she missed a lot of time from her job. I contacted our gynecologist and was grateful that she was able to physically see Jessica in the office. What a blessing! At least now, we could begin to explore what was wrong with her. Jessica had gynecological tests and when the results were all negative, the doctor advised us to pursue GI testing.

As most doctor's offices were closed, this was a huge challenge. Due to the pandemic, our family GI doctor was not accepting new patients, which Jessica would have been. This was understandable, but now I was tasked to find someone who would see her. The Lord blessed us, and we were able to secure another GI doctor. Since most medical appointments were now conducted virtually, we were given an online appointment. Although I have always attended our daughters' medical appointments, doing this online was an additional challenge. I would soon learn that despite this new and wonderful phenomenon, we would often contend with computer system-related difficulties and the obvious fact that the doctor could not physically examine any of us. However, the visit with the doctor went well (of course, I sat next to Jessica to properly communicate with the doctor) and Dr. Mills ordered GI tests for Jessica. Amazingly after one of the tests, which required her to drink liquid barium, her cramping ceased the following day. Just like that. In fact, for weeks, I asked her every day, "Jessica, is your stomach okay?" She would answer, "Still cramping." Now she finally said, "No cramping!" Praise God! We believe that the barium cleared out her colon.

A short time later, it was determined that Jessica had IBSC (Irritable Bowel Syndrome with Constipation). Now having a diagnosis, we were able to modify her diet and she greatly improved. After reading up on IBSC, I will always believe that the pandemic triggered this illness. Stress can precipitate this disorder, and Jessica had never experienced what she was now going through. Now with the cramping gone, Jessica was much better, and we were grateful, as it could have been something far more serious.

During this ordeal, many workers with disabilities, maintained service-related jobs. Often, people with intellectual disabilities have the maturity level of much younger individuals. So in a sense, it was as if children were on the front line being "essential" while many professional workers were staying or working from home. Both Jessica and Jasmine now had to deal with everything "turned upside down" and also adjust to a complete change in their work environments, not to mention their daily lives.

Jessica also had a few other minor health issues. But she handled them like a champ. She burst out crying a couple of times for no apparent reason, but we told her, as we did Jasmine, that crying was good. God gave us the ability to cry for a very good reason, to release our emotions.

ARIE

I too had challenges. I woke up, Sunday morning, 6:00 a.m. on my birthday, April 19, 2020, experiencing terrible stomach pains. God blessed me with the fortitude to make it through playing the keyboard and singing for our church service. After that, I was in bed for the remainder of the day. Later, Charles cooked a wonderful birthday seafood dinner, but I could scarcely eat any of it. What a birthday! Not only that, but this was the early part of the shut-down. Everyone was in shock. Outside of Charles, and Letricia, one of my choir members who sent me a pandemic birthday shirt, I received virtually no gifts and no birthday cards. Why? We were shut down. Most people rarely went to stores. We did not even trust the mail, not knowing if Covid germs were on the mailings. In fact, we would spray the mail we received with a disinfectant. "Drivebys" for birthdays and other celebrations had not yet been created. So, with my health situation and the shutdown, my birthday was completely different. Kinda sad! Although I was in a lot of pain, I was determined not to go to the emergency room.

The next day, I was able to reach our GI doctor, Dr. Chesley, and had a video appointment. He prescribed medication for me, and I had to change my diet to fluids. He determined that my hiatal hernia was the problem. Sometimes, a woman will develop one after receiving a cesarean section and after delivering Jessica, that had apparently happened to me. This was the worst flareup that I had ever experienced, also complicated with the worst case of reflux I had ever had. I'm certain that the stress associated with Covid was responsible. It took weeks for the pain and stomach discomfort to dissipate. During that time, I was tested for Covid which, thank God, was negative. I continued to improve.

In early May, as I was climbing the stairs to our bedroom, I started falling. I grabbed the banister railing and caught myself. In doing so, I injured my left shoulder. It continued to hurt and again, during a shutdown, it was virtually impossible to get basic medical treatments. The first appointment with my orthopedic doctor was a video visit. After more medical facilities reopened, I was able to see the doctor, receive an MRI, and get treatment for small tears in my rotator cuff. I experienced fairly significant pain and had to undergo physical therapy, which helped. Both Jasmine and I were blessed to attend physical therapy located near our house. We were grateful that Dr. Johnson and her physical therapy staff were open to accommodate us, as many medical offices were closed.

CHARLES

As the girls and I experienced our health issues, Charles continued to, as the expression goes, "keep it movin." He continued to be our rock, working on house projects and keeping our church services viable. By his birthday on May 19, 2020, we executed a "drive-by" birthday celebration. "Drive-bys" were now the official means of having family and friends, in person, celebrate occasions such as birthdays and graduations. Cynthia, one of our choir members, and Charles' sister, Rosetta, a godmother of Jessica, helped me organize it. We had a great time, and each facet of his life was represented by family, church members, neighbors, and friends. Later, Charles helped coordinate the "drive-by" birthday we had for Jasmine and Jessica on Sunday, August 30. The front lawn was decorated along with some tables and chairs. Rosetta and other family members, including my cousin Tommy as well as church members, all helped celebrate with Jasmine and Jessica. We were blessed to have family, friends, and neighbors drive by. Some even sat and stayed awhile.

A couple of days later, our family went to our "little white house" in Middlesex County, Virginia. This special house was previously owned by my grandparents. It was the house my mother, Aunt Woncey and their brothers grew up in. So now at this time, it was wonderful to get away. Being the only residents of the house, we had *no* Covid concerns. We were able to go fishing and relax. Charles was in his element. Besides his love for music, hunting and fishing are two of his favorite hobbies. It was great to take a vacation away from so much of the stress of what had again become our "new normal."

Although the news of the day was always death-ridden and politically depressing, we pressed on, just as everyone else did. Pastor Gray continued to lead us with weekly worship services, Bible studies, daily prayer calls, and weekly online prayer services. More people were dying... more reports from far and near...more people whom we knew...more friends dying of the virus as well as other health conditions. Yet we pressed on. Thanksgiving came and Charles helped cook a wonderful meal for just the four of us. We thanked God for getting us through this terrible experience.

As most of us had now learned to use Zoom to conduct business and family celebrations, Charles's family had a Zoom meeting the day after Thanksgiving 2020. It was a great evening, seeing all his siblings, and we began making plans for Christmas gift exchanges. Charles was hunting down in Virginia, staying at our house in Middlesex. With the wonders of technology, he was able to participate in the Zoom call. The girls and I also participated, not realizing how this call would always be held close to our hearts.

On Sunday, during our worship service, Pastor Gray shared with us how grateful he was. He even mentioned the family Zoom call and how amazing it was that *all* of his eight siblings were still alive. The family circle was still intact. We had a wonderful online service, praising God and thanking Him for all our blessings!

A couple hours later, our house phone rang and, recognizing the name on its screen, I immediately answered it. Charles's sister, Joyce, was on the phone, and I could tell that something was very wrong. I yelled for Charles to pick up the other phone extension, and we both listened as she informed us that their sister, Rosetta, had collapsed at a flea market and had been taken to a hospital. She then said these words, "She has already transitioned." I asked, "What do you mean transitioned"? Our world was immediately shaken. The family circle had now been broken. On that unforgettable Sunday afternoon, we did not tell the girls what was going on. We told them that we needed to go and visit someone. They did not need to have this information right now, that their aunt and godmother had gone to be with the Lord. Rosetta was not only my sister-in-law, but for many years, she had been my friend. She had even helped cultivate my relationship with Charles. In a state of shock, Charles and I left our house and quickly drove to the hospital.

Uncannily, Rosetta was taken by ambulance to the same hospital where Mom had died. On our way there, I thought, "Out of all the hospitals in the world, why this one?" Once we went through the hospital's Covid protocols and got to the emergency room door, we saw a few close family members, all bearing the faces of shock and grief. Once inside the ER, we were directed to where she lay lifeless and still. Unbelievably, she was in the exact same area of the emergency room where Mom had laid years before. Some of her sisters were already gathered around her, crying, gently touching her, and consoling one another.

I tried to keep myself together but finally had to leave the room. It was like déjà vu. I felt like I was experiencing Mom's death all over again. I couldn't take it. I was now a wreck. I ran to the waiting room and called Larry to tell him what had happened. I relayed to him that it was like reliving Mom's sudden death: same hospital, same room in the ER, same feeling of shock. He was also stunned. I then had to call and break the news to Marilyn. I then called Andrea & Paul (Geoffrey's godparents). Marilyn and Andrea were both like sisters to Rosetta. We were all devastated!

Charles was a rock. Although he was shocked and grieved at the hospital, he helped all who had gathered to view the body of his departed sister. When we sat down with Jasmine and Jessica that Sunday night, he was the one who told them that Aunt Rosetta was now in heaven with the Lord. I texted their supervisors to let them know what had happened, just in case either one of them might become upset the next day. Two weeks later, we had a funeral for the immediate family and close friends, observing all the Covid protocols. Although there were still hugs of grief and consolation, no one got sick. It was also live-streamed on the Internet. Charles, who officiated the service, did an excellent job and despite our grief, the funeral was beautiful. He continued on, conducting our online church services and Bible studies, and handling all his other responsibilities. He decorated the outside of our house with our usual Christmas lights and helped decorate inside. Despite all that was going on, God continued to grant him strength and peace. Little did we know, as our journey continued, what dangers and challenges loomed ahead.

Chapter 18

JOURNEYING THROUGH THE PANDEMIC

JASMINE

Jasmine was no longer our Jasmine. Normally, she has an outgoing personality and prefers to be with others instead of being alone. Jasmine had insisted that she wanted to attend Rosetta's funeral, so we allowed her to go. Understandably, she was very distraught at the service. Before the service began, she went up to the casket with us. Suddenly, she broke down crying and laid her head on Rosetta's chest. It was very traumatic for her, and for us. I truly understood why Jessica, the day prior had said, "I'm not going," and we did not force her to go.

Although in shock, we "pressed on" and tried to return to our daily new normal. Soon, Jasmine started complaining of headaches. She also complained of drainage in her throat. Believing that she was simply having sinus drainage, I began administering sinus medication to her. We took her blood pressure and discovered that it was becoming more and more elevated. After consulting with our doctors, both Primary Care and Gynecology, they decided soon after Christmas to change the only medication she was taking, which regulated her menstrual cycle.

Christmas 2020 didn't feel like prior Christmases, but I know that it was very different for everyone across the world. Keeping our focus on the real meaning of why we were celebrating helped to provide some facsimile of joy. Rosetta's death had truly been a hard pill to swallow.

Jasmine's supervisor called on the Monday after Christmas, saying that Jasmine was upset and complaining that her throat hurt. Due to Covid-19 protocol, she had to leave her job, as one was not allowed to work with a sore throat. Once Charles brought her home, I took her to urgent care. Since I was also having sinus-related symptoms and didn't feel well myself, both she and I were tested for Covid. The test results were negative. Again, we assumed that her sinuses were causing the drainage problem. Urgent Care prescribed a different sinus medication. Also, the next day she was given (I will refer to it as) "Medication X" by the gynecologist, which replaced her previous medicine. It was hoped that this would regulate her cycle without elevating her blood pressure.

Jasmine continued to have problems. She finally expressed that something was coming up from her chest into her throat. That is when I realized that this was a GI problem and that she was probably having reflux. I immediately contacted our GI doctor, as he had treated Jasmine for this condition some years prior. He ordered tests and fortunately, the only thing they found was that she was having reflux. The stress Jasmine was experiencing had caused this episode, which was substantial. She began taking several medications to stop it, which began to help. A few days later she was able to return to work.

However, she began to act strange and anxious. She began walking differently, her body appearing stiff and leaning in a somewhat backward position. She constantly followed me around. Her demeanor was sad and depressing. She was anxious if Charles and I left her alone in the house for even a short period of time and would frequently call me on my cell phone to ask, "Where are you?" Something was very wrong. The Holy Spirit led me one day to weigh Jasmine and to my dismay, she was down to 85 pounds. Due to the reflux and her apparent reluctance to eat as normal, she had lost twenty pounds. She was thin and walking around the house like a ghost. She was nervous at home and her supervisor advised me that she was very anxious at work. Previously when she was at home, she would sing most of the time. In fact, when I would return from an errand, I could always tell that she had gotten home from work because I could hear her enthusiastically singing in her room. Now, it finally hit me—the singing had stopped. Our daughter was in trouble.

At first, I thought that this was all because of the pandemic, its enormity, and Rosetta's death. I'm sure that all of that caused the reflux to go crazy. But the Lord led me to research online "Medication X" and much to my dismay, there were others who had experienced a major side effect: anxiety. I read numerous accounts of a small percentage of women who, after taking this medication, had suffered from depression, some losing their jobs or relationships. Jasmine was so anxious and nervous on the job that we removed her from work. Her supervisor was very understanding and said that she could take as much time as she needed to get well.

Our primary care physician saw Jasmine in the office and was extremely concerned about her. She decided not to prescribe any type of anti-depressant medication. Instead, she wanted to wait until "Medication X" got out of Jasmine's system, which would take about three months. Thank God, Jasmine slowly began to improve. Also, our gastroenterologist had her on the right regiment of medication. Once the reflux had diminished, Jasmine began to eat more and regain her weight. "Medication X" did take several months to dissipate, and thank God, it did. Jasmine stopped suffering with the anxiety and nervousness she had experienced. She participated with me during my morning devotionals. We read from the book *Jesus Calling*, given to us by Ivory, one of my choir members. It was sent to help us with the healing process of losing Rosetta, and now it was used to help Jasmine heal. We watched Christian broadcasts, e.g. "The 700 Club," and ended this special time together with prayer. Eventually, she started singing again. Thank God!

Despite her improvement, our doctor insisted that Jasmine be evaluated by a mental health professional, just to make certain that she was okay. This was indeed a challenge, especially since all appointments were now virtual. Even though my health insurance company was helpful in assisting me, it was still somewhat difficult to find a psychiatrist who dealt with disabled individuals, especially those with speech challenges. I kept the faith and thankfully, we found a psychiatrist who determined that Jasmine was not suffering from depression. She began meeting online with a friendly therapist and learned strategies for dealing with stress. Jasmine was, as one of our choir's gospel songs proclaims, "On the Right Road Now" and was soon fully recovered. Thank God!

Jasmine's Workplace During the Pandemic

JESSICA

Jessica continued to work and perform well. She has always gotten along well with her co-workers and has had understanding supervisors. God has continued to keep her safe, and overall, she has maintained a high level of happiness. She has continued to plan for our next cruise. We assured her that someday we will go on another cruise, and although the industry had not returned to normal, Jessica still searched the Internet for updated information. She even texted us links, which made us smile, knowing that she had not given up her desire to travel on the high seas. One day, I noticed a black luggage bag near her bed. Upon opening it, I found tightly packed clothes and shoes, including flip flops. I said, "Jessica, what is all of this?" She simply replied, "For the cruise." Bless her heart! She was a great example of demonstrating hope, which the Lord wants all of us to have. Hopefully next year, the pandemic would be over.

ARIE

Around the time Jasmine started having reflux, I found myself having the same GI symptoms as before. It appeared that my medication was no longer working, and I again had to contact our doctor. He prescribed another medication and ironically, I was now taking exactly the same medicines that Jasmine ended up being prescribed. Although this GI situation was bothersome, there was no comparison to the upcoming dangerous situation that almost occurred.

On the Friday night of December 18, 2020, I stayed up late watching television. Charles had gone down to Virginia at about 4:00 a.m. that morning to hunt for most of the weekend. It was a week after Rosetta's funeral, Jasmine and Jessica had gone to bed, and it was now about 1:30 a.m. When Charles is away, I admit, I don't feel as secure. We do have a burglar alarm but still, I decided to go downstairs to make certain the door leading to the garage was locked. I decided to use the elevator. In the years since Dad was gone, we mainly used it for transporting musical equipment and luggage. But on this night, I chose to ride in it, downstairs and back.

When I left the bedroom to go downstairs, I headed down the dark hallway toward the elevator. I pushed the button and did not hear it come from another floor, which meant that it was already on my level. I opened the door and started to step into the dark elevator and turn on its light. Suddenly, a voice in my head yelled, "Stop!!" I obeyed, stopped, and stepped back. The voice inside my head said, "Turn on the hall light." I immediately went over to the hall light switch. Shockingly, when I switched on the light and turned back to look at the elevator, I realized that *it was not there!* There must have been a massive malfunction because the elevator car was all the way down to the basement level. As I stood near the elevator door, I could see empty space and cables.

I ran back to our bedroom, grabbed my cell phone which had a flashlight app, and returned to the would-be disaster. The flashlight revealed the ceiling of the elevator car down below, seemingly made of cement and steel bolts. I had never seen anything like this before. I stood there looking down at it in shock, realizing that if I had stepped into the elevator, I would more than likely have died. This was indeed divine intervention! In my head, the Holy Spirit had actually yelled at me to stop. Lord have mercy! I closed the elevator door and went back to our bedroom in a state of shock. Just thinking about what almost happened shook me to my core. I thought of how Charles was not there, how the girls were asleep, and God only knows the enormity of what almost happened. I was so shaken that it took me several hours before I was able to go to sleep. I thanked God for what He did. This near-death experience affected me so that initially, I shared it only with a few people. It was so traumatic! Even thinking of it now brings tears to my eyes.

I used this experience as a teaching tool for Jasmine and Jessica. I told them that whenever you prepare to get onto an elevator, make sure that it is safe before you walk into it. When Charles came home, he could not make the elevator malfunction again. A technician came out, inspected it, and again, could not get the elevator to repeat the malfunction. In fact, he had never heard of that happening. However, he did conduct a minor repair. Later in May of 2021, Jessica had an injury and began using the elevator on a regular basis. Even though the elevator was inspected and repaired, we reminded the girls about elevator safety. The Lord has also encouraged me to begin sharing this near-death experience with others. Why? Because we need God; we need to be in tune with the Holy Spirit and in this case with the elevator; it was a matter of life and death. I am so grateful that the Lord saved me and that I was obedient to His voice.

As the pandemic continued, one of my biggest concerns was obtaining the vaccine. Jasmine was able to get her shot at her job. To my dismay, it was taking a longer time for Jessica to receive a vaccine. My concern was that we as a family, with Charles and my health issues, needed both of our daughters vaccinated as soon as possible.

But God! One morning, as my frustration increased trying to get Jessica vaccinated, the Lord convicted me to spend more time with Him. I had gotten in a habit of having morning devotionals while watching Christian programming on TV. However, on this particular Monday morning, which was President's Day, I was about to skip this time with the Lord and delve into the vaccine matter. Interestingly, it was as if I was being pulled back and reminded to resume my routine of spending "alone time" with the Lord. So obediently, I did just that, and I believe it made a positive difference.

After my quiet time with the Lord, I went to my computer. The "little voice" told me to contact EPIC, the agency that supports Jasmine, Jessica, and other adults with disabilities. I informed them of Jessica's vaccine status, and copied their disability service agency's CEO, who quickly responded. She stated that Jessica could be vaccinated along with their clients in residential housing on February 22. Glory be to God!

Later that evening, I then began surfing the Internet, checking several venues, trying to acquire a vaccine for myself. Jasmine was sitting next to me, watching me as I pursued what I figured would be an impossible feat. Previously, I had registered through our state and nearby hospitals. Nothing! So many people wanted vaccines and the wait was problematic. But the Lord intervened. Soon, I found myself on our nearby grocery store's website and ventured to the Covid vaccine page. Within a few clicks, followed by completing the necessary fields of personal data, I was now viewing a screen that displayed a calendar to click on to reserve a date for receiving the vaccine. The February calendar was completely grey, which indicated that there was no availability. I advanced to the next screen for March and continued through September, only to find nothing.

I started to "X" out of the window, but the "little voice" told me to go back. I went backwards, one month at a time until I reached February. To my surprise, February 28 suddenly changed, right before our eyes, from the color grey to green. In disbelief, Jasmine and I looked at each other, and I quickly clicked on the date. Within a few seconds, my appointment was confirmed. I told Jasmine that she had witnessed something very special and that the "little voice" had told me to go back. I didn't close out my screen. Instead, I obeyed, and now, I was scheduled for a greatly desired vaccine. I remembered that the Lord had drawn me to Him so I could spend time with Him, and I had complied. Not only did He lead me to acquire Jessica's vaccine appointment, but He also blessed me with my own.

CHARLES

Charles had his hands full taking care of us and grieving the loss of his sister. But he was still our rock, a steady boat navigating turbulent waters. He was also very concerned about Jasmine. No one outside of our household really understood the mental state she was in. Then on March 8, I accidentally got some detergent in my right eye. After hours of discomfort and a call to the poison control folks, I was advised to go to the ER because one of the chemicals could possibly cause permanent eye damage. Charles took me to a nearby hospital, only five minutes away. After a long wait, it was determined that I had no eye damage; I was prescribed an eye drop to use and told to take acetaminophen for pain. We gratefully returned home.

The next day, March 9, began as uneventful, but it was still a pandemic day. By then, Jasmine was doing much better, and my eye was improving. It was late that afternoon that Charles called me on my cell phone, asking me to come upstairs to his office. I thought that he wanted to show me something on his computer. Once there, I saw that he was sitting in his recliner and beckoned me to sit in a chair beside him. He took my hand and stated, "I don't feel well." Mind you, my husband never, ever gets sick. I was quickly alarmed, asking what his symptoms were. He said, "I feel lightheaded. I just don't feel right."

By now, it was time to eat dinner. I thought that if he ate, he might feel better. Instead, upon eating only one fork full of food, the words "I think I need to go to the hospital," came from his mouth. I was stunned but quickly gathered myself to take him to the ER. After shouting instructions to the girls, yet trying to remain calm, I helped him walk to the garage to get into the car. He told me that his left arm felt heavy as did his left leg. I suspected that he was having a stroke and fear gripped my body. As he was having difficulty even lifting his foot into the car, I knew that this was bad. Though I got him seated, I yanked my cell phone out of my purse and called 911. Once they answered and began asking questions, though appropriate, I cancelled the call by hanging up. The hospital was virtually within walking distance and if he was having a stroke, every moment was critically important. Driving him myself was the quickest way to get him there.

When we got to the hospital, I ran in and stated that my husband needed care at once, that he might be having a stroke. An attendant pushing a wheelchair came outside with me, helped Charles get into the wheelchair, and took him in. Hurriedly, I went to park the car. At 6:42 p.m., I called Minister Harley, and told him what was going on. Charles was supposed to conduct a meeting of a pastoral group he had created, and

Minister Harley needed to fill in for him. He assured me that he would take care of the meeting, that they would pray for Pastor, and he encouraged me to be as calm as possible.

I returned to the waiting area but was now in somewhat of a panic mode. The hospital staff seemed to move so slowly. I insisted that someone check him out, which they did. I did not want to offend any of them, especially since we needed them more than they needed us. So, we waited in the waiting room. At 8:15, Charles looked across the room at the clock, then turned to me and said, "You know, I feel like something just lifted off me. I feel great. I feel like I could play a game of basketball." I softly whispered in his ear, "Shut up." Yes, I did! Although I had never told him that before, I did so now because I did *not* want any of the staff to hear him. I wanted them to run all the tests needed to determine what had happened to my dear husband. Finally, they took him back to the ER but due to Covid restrictions, I could not go with him. Charles quickly advised me to return home and wait there until he called me.

Later, after Charles called, I returned to the hospital, and he was discharged. After running various tests, they had found no evidence of a stroke. They told him to take a baby aspirin twice a day and see a neurologist as soon as possible. They also advised him to follow up with his primary care doctor and cardiologist. We were exhausted but gratefully returned home.

The next day, Charles' brother Bernard came by to check on him. Due to the pandemic, he sat in the middle of the front yard and Charles talked to him from the front porch. While they were talking, "something" made Charles look at his text messages from the night before. He noticed that one of the pastors from the Tuesday night meeting, who was from the Billy Graham Evangelistic Association, had texted him at 8:12. One of his last sentences informed Charles that, "People from all across the world are praying for you." It was at that point that my husband realized the timing of the message. Remember, at 8:15 he had told me that something lifted from him and that he felt great. He told Bernard, "Brother, you won't believe this" and proceeded to tell him that the Lord had indeed answered prayers for his healing. The power of prayer!

Within a few days, Charles was seen by a neurologist. He was also seen by our cardiologist, and wore a heart monitor for a week. After all the neurological and cardiological tests along with MRIs, no evidence of a stroke was found. He was scheduled to have more tests in a few months and remain on the blood thinner that the neurologist had prescribed.

Charles was quite elated that I, his "ball and chain" would no longer have to accompany him on simple errands. That's right! When he had his first appointment with the neurologist, the doctor cautioned him that until he had completed all his tests, he should not operate a boat alone, swim alone, and that it would be better if he were accompanied while driving a motor vehicle. So, I stuck to him, as my mom used to say, like "white on rice." My husband has always been very independent, so this was indeed a major adjustment for him. I didn't mind because I love him, and this actually allowed us to spend more time together. I literally made him slow down. "Look," I said, "the things that you don't need to do right now can wait. I know that you wanted to get the new church location ready by Easter Sunday, but your health is more important." He reluctantly agreed. He had been doing some renovations, but now was indeed *not* the time.

Everyone was ecstatic that he was doing well, but just as Charles was adjusting to this slow period, things suddenly got very busy. He, wearing his other "hat" as real estate agent, had listed Aunt Woncey's house, affectionately named "Mapleshade," located in Burgess, Virginia. Aunt Woncey had moved most of her things to her daughter's house in Richmond, Virginia. Now, a rare time in his life when he was supposed to be taking it easy, someone had submitted a contract on her home. Of course, we were all happy for her. But it required work on Charles' part, including settlement of a few complications regarding the property. Finally, on Monday, March 22nd, the closing was held at 1:00 p.m. Burgess was only a little over two hours away and although my husband said, "You don't have to go," I simply ignored him. I was not going to let him travel and perform everything he needed to accomplish alone. One final issue surfaced. A company that serviced the house needed to certify a utility issue that morning at 7:00 a.m. So, we crawled out of bed and left our house at 4:15. Despite a couple of unexpected delays, we got to Burgess at 6:55 and the gentleman from the company arrived at 7:10. We thanked God for perfect timing!

The remainder of the morning was somewhat emotional for us. Mapleshade consisted of this charming country home, embellished by glorious shade trees and peaceful surroundings. It held a lot of memories, and as I walked from room to room, tears flowed from my eyes. I thought of Uncle T, who had gone to be with the Lord in 2011. My mind recalled moments from the past...the wonderful life he, Aunt Woncey and my dear cousins, Tommy, Nerissa and George had shared here. It was as if another chapter of my life was leaving me. Charles hugged me and confessed that he felt the same way. Each year, after we were married, he would drive down to the Northern Neck of Virginia to hunt deer and stay at Mapleshade. I went outside, stopped crying, and reminded myself that this was for the best. Aunt Woncey had been wanting this to happen for many years and was relieved that the wait for selling her house was finally over. We met her at the real estate office for the closing, which because of Covid, took place in the parking lot. Soon, the papers were all signed. After exchanging air kisses, we left for our trip home, which ended up being much different than we could have anticipated.

When we got to Westmoreland County, Virginia, Charles pulled the truck into the parking lot of a gas station and the Birddogs Country Store. Although I was tempted to go in for some snacks, I stayed in the truck. Charles had a taste for fresh oysters, and this store carried some of the best. A few minutes later, he came out, turned the key in the ignition, and the truck would not start. After several attempts, the truck still would not start. Great! So, we waited, hoping that soon, things would change. They didn't. "Can you believe this?" Charles asked. Now, we were indeed frustrated but knew that getting upset would not solve anything. Little did we know that God had another plan. In retrospect, despite the circumstances, we received several blessings.

The first was that customers from the store tried desperately to help us. We were there at least 3½ hours. Almost everyone who entered and left the store was Caucasian. Very few African-Americans were customers. Why was this significant to me? During this time period, our country was extremely challenged, to say the least. Race relations, as expressed by many, had continued to deteriorate. After George Floyd was killed by the actions of police officers in May of 2020, protests and looting in various cities became the norm. There was turmoil throughout the land. Charles and I did not "buy into" the disdain that some expressed towards white people, as we know that most people are decent human beings. But the racial atmosphere had shifted to a negative state of being, which, compounded by all the trauma of Covid-19, was simply terrible. Yet, here we were, with total strangers stopping to help and asking Charles to describe the truck's symptoms. While I went in to purchase some snacks, one gentleman called his son-in-law to see if he could tow us back to Maryland. Unfortunately, his son-in-law had already gone to Waldorf, Maryland, which is in the neighboring county to us, only twenty minutes away from our home. Some folks tried whatever they could think of to perform under the truck's hood, hoping to solve the problem. Nothing worked. However, it was a reminder that most people *are* good people, and they took their time to come to our aid, which they did *not* have to do. One of the store's employees even came out and gave me a bag of chips, to add to the snacks I had already purchased.

The last gentleman who stopped to help us was African-American. He even physically climbed up to inspect under the hood. Charles told him to be careful so he would not hurt himself. The man was an interesting-looking person, with long mixed grey dregs. What was most incredible was his name, Lawrence Johnson, the same name as Dad's, spelled exactly the same! He talked with us for almost an hour, and we found that we knew some of the same people there in the area. As a hunter, Lawrence also exchanged hunting information with Charles. At one point, as we relayed our frustration over this ordeal, he remarked, "God did not want you to be on the road right now." Charles looked at him and replied, "I believe that you are right." I also believed exactly what Lawrence had said.

Charles called for roadside assistance and finally, the towing company came. This part of the story was the second blessing. The tow truck driver was Caucasian, and again, very personable. Charles tried to start the truck once more, just in case we did *not* have to be towed. Of course, the truck would not cooperate. As the driver began to load the truck onto the flatbed, Charles told me that since the truck only had a front seat, the company may not permit both of us to ride. If the driver refused to let us both ride, that would create a big logistical problem for us. Fortunately, he let us both ride. Thank God! I sat as close to Charles as I could. Due to Covid, I did not feel comfortable sitting as close as I was to the driver, but I had no choice. Social distancing could not be done here. I just had to continue to trust God for protection. The driver revealed that he had been vaccinated, which made me feel a little more comfortable. As we talked, wearing our masks of course, we soon discovered that we knew a lot of the same people in Middlesex County, Virginia. It was amazing! The three of us had a great conversation. Our driver had told us back at the country store that he would not be surprised if the truck started once we reached our destination. He said that sometimes after a long ride filled with vibrations, the vehicle will start. We hoped his prediction was incorrect. We wanted Sheldon, our mechanic, to properly determine, what was wrong. This time we did *not* want the truck to start. We continued to talk, including comments on the importance of a belief in God. Hopefully, we made a positive impact on the driver.

At about 7:45 p.m., we finally arrived at Sheldon's shop. They got the truck off the flatbed and Charles decided to see if it would start. He turned the key in the ignition, and you guessed it. The driver's prediction was correct. It started. I felt like running over to the truck and kicking it. Charles relayed to Sheldon the sentiments of the people back at the country store—that it was probably the fuel pump. The next morning, Sheldon determined that their sentiments were correct.

We were more than ready to leave. Sheldon told us that one of his drivers would take us home. Thank God! We transferred items from our truck to the driver's truck. I sat in the back seat and was relieved that we were finally on our way home. Now came our third blessing. Charles proceeded to talk to the young man now driving us and we were immediately impressed with his manners. Upon Charles' questioning, he expressed his feelings about the Lord, his life, and his ambitions. As we told him about our day, beginning with being in the Northern Neck, he began to recall his childhood memories of being there, specifically in Burgess, Virginia! He used to go to Taylor's beach and was related to the Taylor family. Why was this amazing? We knew his family. Uncle T had conducted a yearly baptism at Taylor's beach for 40 years. By the time we found out our commonalities, we were now in front of our house. I called Aunt Woncey and put her on speaker phone so she could also speak with this personable young man. They realized that she knew his grandmother very well. After we ended the conversation with her, Charles continued to talk with him and witnessed to him about how God wanted to bless his life. As I took some of our belongings into the house, I marveled about the things that had transpired. Yes, I was exhausted. It had been a very long day. It was 8:30 p.m. and the "ball and chain" was, as we used to say, "beat." But I still had some pep in my step. I remembered that Lawrence Johnson, as he conversed with us, had said "God doesn't want you to be on the road right now." I smiled. Charles and I will always believe that the Lord protected us from unseen danger.

In the days that passed, Charles continued to be symptom-free. We went to the cardiologist to find out the results from him wearing the heart monitor. Everything was fine. His blood pressure was so good that the doctor decreased his blood pressure medication. The following week, we went back to the neurologist and again, received an excellent report. All tests were negative. The doctor said, "Mr. Gray, I recommend that you continue to take the blood thinner for the next two months, and we will repeat your Electroencephalogram (EEG) at that time." Charles Gray was doing well, and the "ball and chain" was now free. We were so happy and to celebrate, we went to the National Harbor for a late lunch. Although everyone was still wearing masks and social distancing, we were very happy. We knew we were going to make it!

Chapter 19

THE PANDEMIC CONTINUES

JASMINE

Jasmine returned to work on May 14, 2021. She went back to being Jasmine and it was such a joy to see her smiling face. Her supervisor and co-workers were happy to see her back at work. I had a virtual appointment with our primary care doctor on May 27, which was a day when Jasmine was not scheduled to work. I had her say hello to Dr. Norwood so that she could see Jasmine's progress. Our doctor, who was still very much concealed in her PPE's, was pleased to speak with our daughter. Jasmine said, "Thank you so much for helping me." She also used the sign language for "thank you" and our doctor said "Jasmine, you have really made my day." After Jasmine left the room, I told Dr. Norwood, "I did not tell her to say that to you." She replied "I know you didn't. You have such a sweet daughter. I know that what she said was from the heart."

Jasmine went back to singing and praise dancing (liturgical dancing used to worship God). On the days she wasn't scheduled to work, she still remembered to read with me during my devotional time and enjoyed our prayer time together. Soon, when I returned home from errands, I began again to know when Jasmine was in the house. I could hear her singing again. Praise God!

JESSICA

On the Thursday morning prior to Memorial Day, 2021, I noticed that Jessica was limping, just before leaving the house to go to work. I questioned her, had her sit down, and show me what part of her foot was bothering her. The area was the fatty part of the bottom of her foot at the base of her big toe. I ran upstairs and applied a bunion cushion to help give her foot some padding. It seemed to work, and she went on her way. I made sure she kept the pad on, but then the next morning, one of her supervisors called me. Jessica was limping at work, and they were afraid she would fall. So, Charles went to get her. I quickly contacted our podiatrist's office. Due to Covid, their schedule was full, and they could not see her right away. Thank God, due to a cancellation, I was able to take her within a couple of days to their office.

After Jessica's foot was x-rayed, we went to the examination room and waited. Soon, Dr. Hotchkiss and his assistant came in. It was good to see him, as we had not seen him since 2019. He examined her foot and applied pressure to the area in question, which caused her obvious pain. Then he turned to me and stated, "Mrs. Gray, Jessica has a broken bone in her foot." I replied, "What? Are you serious?" He said, "Yes." I told him that I was shocked! He then showed me the x-ray and discussed what is called a sesamoid bone. I couldn't believe it! The doctor asked Jessica if she had fallen, and she replied, "No." He then stated that you can easily break this bone simply by stepping off a street curb the wrong way.

After the diagnosis, Jessica had to wear an orthopedic boot, but she worked every day and handled the situation well. In fact, in July, she was "Employee of the Month" at her job, boot and all! We were proud of her. Her foot status was concerning because the sesamoid bone is a very difficult one to heal. We prayed that she would ultimately not have to have surgery. Finally, by September, we received another blessing. She was fully healed. "Ms. Boot," as we affectionately called her, was finally back to normal, still searching the Internet for cruise information!

Jessica, Employee of the Month

ARIE

There's an old saying, "When it rains, it pours." I began experiencing substantial pain in my right hip in January 2021. This continued for months and I began limping around the house. Charles told me "Please go to the doctor," and finally, I did. Our orthopedic doctor told me that the pain was coming from my back. He referred me to physical therapy, and it helped somewhat. Then I received an MRI, which showed the true condition of my lower back. The MRI revealed a lot of degeneration, which could have resulted from scoliosis (a curvature that had been diagnosed when I was a teenager) and the multiple automobile accidents I had experienced over the years. My physical therapist and doctor recommended that I seek pain management therapy. The pain management doctor reviewed and explained the MRI to me. He would conduct a series of procedures that would hopefully eliminate most, if not all of my pain.

CHARLES

Charles continued to do well. During the first week of April 2021, he received a Covid-19 vaccine. We were grateful that he had not received it prior to his stroke-like episode, as we may have assumed that the vaccine was responsible for his symptoms. The Lord continued to sustain us, and we had our first worship service in our new facility on the first Sunday in June. What a blessing! Although there were only 10 of us, it was wonderful. Thereafter, a slowly increasing number of members returned. We practiced social distancing, sanitization, and wore masks. We had truly been blessed in so many ways!

GEOFFREY

Geoffrey, who has been living in North Carolina for a number of years, had not been back home since Mother's Day, 2019. Not counting video chatting on the phone, that was the last time that we had seen him. So when his work schedule allowed him to come home, he arrived on Friday night, September 17, 2021.

I had some reservations, as I was almost positive that he had not been vaccinated. I had discussed my views with him for months and at one point, he stated that he would take the vaccine. But I suspected he hadn't. So now I was torn as to what to do. Should I tell him not to come, to come wearing a mask, or simply trust in God's protection? I chose the last option.

We were so glad to see him! It had been so long. He told us that he had been tested recently for Covid and seemed fine. However, on Saturday, he said he had slept very poorly that Friday night, and that his back was hurting him. I gave him some anti-inflammatory cream for his back and some over-the-counter pain medicine. He felt better and decided to go get his car washed. He had named his car Gloria, and I happily rode to the car wash with him.

By early Monday evening, he said, "Mom, I don't feel well," and asked me to take his temperature. It was indeed elevated. Thirty minutes later, it was even higher. Charles took him to Urgent Care, but they were unable to test him for Covid. There were too many people to be seen within the hour before their 8:00 p.m. closing time. Charles and Geoffrey came back home. Ultimately, Geoffrey insisted upon driving himself to the hospital because now, he didn't want to be in close proximity to any of us. He went to the hospital, was tested, and yes, tested positive for Covid-19!

The news was devastating and surreal at the same time. Around 2:00 a.m., Geoffrey returned from the ER and said that he would leave that morning. He did not want to further expose us and after getting some sleep, prepared to leave. We were now wearing our masks, but we knew that we had been severely exposed. I hated the fact that he was sick and going to attempt a 6-to-7-hour drive, but he said he would be okay. He lived alone and knew that friends would drop off food for him outside his door. His departure was very emotional, as he was upset with himself and the entire situation. Charles calmly told him that he had to focus on safely getting home. We never chastised him about not getting the vaccine. He was sick and needed prayer. We prayed for him and reminded him that we loved him. Thank God, he made it back home safely. He told me on Wednesday, that if he had waited one more day, he would not have had the strength to drive back home to North Carolina. We were grateful that the Lord had given him strength, protection and grace.

Now we had to face all the consequences, beginning with the cancellation of scheduled doctors' appointments. The girls were both at home, as they were supposed to have had physical exams that afternoon. Charles and I isolated them to their rooms that Tuesday morning and took food to them. Then he, even more than I, did his best to sanitize the house, especially the areas that Geoffrey had frequented. I immediately contacted Jasmine and Jessica's supervisors and asked about their quarantine protocol, which was now 10 days long. Our family was now under quarantine and our lives had changed, yet again.

Based on CDC (Center for Disease Control) guidelines, we knew that we must wait a while to be tested. So, we decided to make the best of a bad situation. I said to Charles, "How about we go to Middlesex?" He looked at me, smiled and quickly said, "Start packing." We took care of all our communications, responsibilities and appointments, and then explained the situation to the girls. Although I had told Jasmine and Jessica that they would be out of work for the next two weeks, the Holy spirit told me that they did not really understand what was going on. So, I had to explain what quarantine was and what we were having to do. I also explained the concept of turning "lemons into lemonade" and that is what the Middlesex trip was going to do for us. We had a great time and went fishing on our boat twice. Both Jasmine and Jessica caught a number of fish and again, we had a lot of fun in the midst of the chaos of Covid. I made appointments for us to be tested on the following Tuesday afternoon back at our nearby CVS drugstore.

I continued to keep in communication with Geoffrey, who was doing well and was not deathly sick. He had not encountered serious problems with breathing, had lost his sense of smell for only one day, and planned to get retested. He hoped that a negative test would allow him soon to return to his job.

None of us had any symptoms. Praise God! We returned home on Tuesday and got tested. I had requested the PCR test, which is more accurate, and we all did our tests inside the car. I got in the back seat with Jasmine and Jessica so that I could do the swab test for them. It was a little uncomfortable, but we did fine. We were informed by the CVS employee who administered the test, that we would be notified in a day or two. After getting back home and settling down, I found myself in a bit of a "strange place." I went to our family room, sat down, and the next thing I knew, I was crying. So much had been going on—and now this. Every day we were hearing about violence or death, even the deaths of people we knew. In that moment, it wasn't that I didn't trust God. I was simply grieved by the enormity of so much going on and was also feeling the grief of others. Also, as a mom, my heart ached! It was unbelievable that my dear children were having to go through this insane pandemic. Jasmine, my "shadow" came in and sat down beside me. I could feel her looking at me, so I stopped crying. I reminded her that crying was okay, and that Mommy was fine. We then began watching one of our favorite TV cooking shows. Both Jasmine and Jessica are very sensitive to the feelings of others, and I knew that if I kept crying, Jasmine would start crying herself. I knew I had to continue to trust God and keep the faith. We would be fine.

Within two days, the results came in. We had all tested *negative*! We were so happy and grateful. Geoffrey experienced lingering soreness and fatigue, but overall, handled Covid well. God blessed us all!

After this Covid scare, life continued. I had been suffering from back pain starting in January 2021, and it continued to worsen. Although I tried physical therapy and pain management, relief proved to be temporary. I went to see the doctor who had operated on Charles in early 2019, and he scheduled surgery to occur on November 17, 2021. I contemplated slowing down the process and waiting until early

2022, but that would have been a huge mistake. Why, because unfortunately, another Covid variant emerged, named *Omicron.* Hospitals were filling up yet again. I personally experienced this reality in October.

It was a little after midnight. I had a multitude of symptoms, which included extremely elevated blood pressure, dizziness and shortness of breath. Charles called 911. Soon, the EMTs arrived and through chattering teeth, as I felt a sense of coldness that I had never before experienced, I answered the questions they asked me as best I could. As I was lying there on the stretcher, I realized that the EMT was having to call multiple hospitals, searching for one that would accept me. Although we live five minutes from a hospital, they were directed to bypass it as well as other neighboring hospitals, and we ended up going to Northern Virginia. As they conducted various tests on me in the ambulance, we whizzed in and out of traffic. I thought about how crazy this was that because of overcrowding, I could not go to hospitals closer to where we lived. That was indeed a wake-up call, reminding us of the fact that the ongoing pandemic was still very real.

Charles got to the hospital soon after I was taken to the ER. He told me that although Jasmine and Jessica were understandably upset, they would be fine. After running tests on me, everything checked out. My blood pressure greatly improved, they gave me medication for my back, which by now was really painful, and then they discharged me. The only medical conclusion was that I had experienced a very severe reaction to a flu shot I received earlier that day. I had taken the flu shot every year for decades and never had experienced this type of reaction. I rested for several days and finally began to feel better. Months later, it was confirmed that the flu shot I had been given, formulated for people over 65, was apparently too strong for me. I did not know that there are different flu vaccines, and I now know which one to request to prevent that from happening again.

Despite that experience, it did not hinder me from undergoing the lower back surgery I had scheduled for November 17. My surgeon had operated on both our next-door neighbor and Charles. So, I felt comfortable letting this doctor perform the operation on my back. Thank God the surgery went well. Physical therapy would begin in a couple of months.

A short time later in 2021, it was Thanksgiving yet again, and the dinner consisted of only the four of us. Since I had recently had back surgery, Joyce and Elsie, two of Charles' sisters, brought over a delicious Thanksgiving dinner. We had a joyous Thanksgiving and later, a wonderful Christmas. Our entire family was healed, and I was improving each day. Although Geoffrey had some residual symptoms from Covid, he was grateful, as it could have been so much worse.

Again, we spent New Year's Eve at home. Unlike so many years, 2020 and 2021 New Year's Eves held more uncertainty than ever before. But we reflected on how the Lord had safely brought us through another year of Covid-19. The Lord had indeed blessed us. He protected us. I could truly say that I had hugged Covid, rode in the car with Covid (I'm referring to Geoffrey's September visit), and still did not catch this disease. Since New Year's Day was that Saturday, and Covid was still an issue, we did not have a New Year's Eve Service. Pastor let our fellowship know that we would have Sunday worship service online, including communion. So, unlike previous New Year's Eve nights, the four of us held hands around the kitchen table, right before midnight. We reflected on God's grace; Charles led us in prayer, and each of us expressed something that we were grateful for. We ended this special time by embracing each other. Although I experienced that feeling of apprehension I felt every year at this time, I knew that the Lord would see us through. Another Covid variant or a new crisis might lie ahead, and little did I know how God would protect us yet again!

Chapter 20

DELIVERANCE FROM EVIL

Wow, a brand-new year and the Covid pandemic continued! On January 2, 2022, we had our first Sunday worship service of the New Year online, which proved to be a blessing. Why? Because Jessica started showing signs of illness with a scratchy throat on that Monday. Simultaneously, we had a snowstorm and thankfully, Jasmine and Jessica were not scheduled to work that day. I reported Jessica's illness to her supervisor, so that he would not expect Jessica at work until we knew that she did not have Covid. Due to the enormous number of sick people, the urgent care centers were not allowing anyone to come in for Covid testing. I did not have home test kits, and there was a shortage of these tests. Nor could we get her tested at our doctor's office.

Fortunately, the Lord provided. That Wednesday, I went next door to the home of Rev. Parrish to drop off a belated Christmas gift. Due to the ongoing pandemic, we met at the end of her snowy driveway. To my surprise, her Christmas gift to me was a set of Covid test kits, just what we needed! I told her that Jessica was sick and that she really needed testing before returning to work, hopefully, the next day.

I immediately tested Jessica and sure enough, the test quickly displayed that she was positive for Covid! I was shocked and immediately called Charles, who was at the grocery store. He wanted to take her to an urgent care facility, and I proceeded to spend hours, unsuccessfully, trying to get an appointment. I also gave her another test, just to make sure. Again, she tested positive. It was a good thing that she was tested, as she was feeling better and I would have allowed her to return to work, thinking that her symptoms were allergy related. Again, I was shocked. God had protected us for so long from Covid. It was hard to believe.

I called Charles again and told him about the second test result. Then I proceeded to prepare for Jessica's quarantine, as well as the impact it would have on our daily routine. Fortunately, Jessica did not have a fever. Her only symptoms were a scratchy throat and periodic dry cough. Due to military Covid protocols, as Jessica works for the Marines, she would need to stay home for a couple of weeks. Because Jasmine worked for the Army, she also needed to stay home from work. Fortunately, neither Jasmine, Charles, nor I tested positive for Covid.

Jessica enjoyed her time alone. Since she prefers to be in her room, she was ecstatic! The scratchy throat lasted for only about a week and overall, she felt fine. We delivered food to her on a tray outside her door, and she got to eat her favorites. She was very happy. In fact, she was probably the happiest person with Covid in the DMV. She didn't have to go to work and had a great time—watching TV, eating in her room, and playing on her computer. What's not to enjoy!

Because of our quarantine, on the following Sunday, we conducted our church service again online. It was during the service that I found out something disturbing having to do with Jasmine. One of our church members had a technical problem with his computer and could not access our service online. So, he called me on my cell phone and asked if I could keep his call open on my phone so that he could listen to our service. "Sure," I said. However, I needed to communicate with our assistant minister to make certain that the volume levels of our service transmission were satisfactory. I couldn't use Pastor Gray's phone, as other listeners who did not have computers or only had landline phones called his cell to listen to the service. So, I borrowed Jasmine's phone and texted Minister Harley to verify sound levels. Afterwards, as I listened to Pastor relay some church announcements, something made me scroll through Jasmine's cell phone, viewing her phone apps (applications). I noticed that Jasmine had Cash App on her phone, which is a popular mobile payment service. I have it on my phone but why did she? She and Jessica were not supposed to have this app on their phones. I opened it, and to my shock, realized that she had been sending money to someone. I was stunned, as neither Jasmine nor Jessica was supposed to be engaging in this type of activity. After our church service, I showed it to Charles and both of us questioned her. We discovered that she had indeed, for the past several months, been sending money to another employee, whom we will call Lee. This individual had taken advantage of Jasmine's naivety, trust, and generosity.

I then began to research the entire situation and found messages on a text stream between Lee and Jasmine. It was evident that Lee knew that what was going on was wrong and repeatedly texted Jasmine not to tell us about it. I was angry with the employee and disappointed with Jasmine. To provide documented evidence, I had to produce a lot of screenshots from Lee's texts and Cash App transaction screens. The "little voice" told me a short time later to retrieve Jasmine's phone from her again and investigate all her text messages. To my shock, I found yet another text stream with even more incriminating messages from Lee. I realized that God had enabled me to find all the messages between the two of them. Once I conveyed the documentation that proved what had transpired, Jasmine's employer contacted Lee's family, and the family agreed to reimburse Jasmine for the money that she had sent to Lee.

This situation served as a reminder to all of us to monitor our children's phones and computers, special needs or not. Yes, as they tend to be very trusting, people can easily take advantage of special needs youth. However, this can happen to anyone, young and old alike.

After several weeks, the situation with Lee was officially resolved and we would soon become victims of not one crime, but two. A few months prior to the situation with Jasmine, Charles began renovating the house we used to live in. It was the house that we called home, that the girls and Geoffrey grew up in as little children. He, along with other hired workers, did a fantastic job and the house looked beautiful. It was even more gorgeous than it was when we had lived there. Charles worked so hard with the assistance of his brother Bernard. Near the end of January, on a Friday, Charles put the house on the market to be sold. Realtors began showing it the very next day. On that Monday afternoon, a real estate agent called Charles. The agent said he wanted to show the house to a client, but the lockbox was missing from the front door. (A lockbox is a metal padlock shaped box that usually hangs from the door handle of a house that is on the market so that real estate agents can enter the home.) Charles thanked the agent and immediately tried to understand how this could have happened. Lockboxes are very secure and almost impossible to steal or pry loose.

A short time later, Charles went to the house. Not only was the lockbox missing, but his house key would not open the door. To his dismay, he realized that someone, through the back door, had broken into the house and changed the locks on all the doors. That was how the lockbox had been removed. The criminals removed the entire doorknob, which the lockbox had been attached to. They also removed the "For Sale" sign from the front lawn. Unbelievable! Charles called the police, and they searched the house to make sure that no one was hiding on the premises. Charles made a few repairs and installed new locks on the doors. Soon afterwards, he found a letter in the outside mailbox from our county's utility company, welcoming a woman (someone we did *not* know) at that address as a new customer. Obviously, the criminals planned to have someone move into our house. We learned that this unfortunate scenario is being played out across our country, and it can take many months to legally get the inhabitants removed. Due to the pandemic, court cases were backlogged so only God knows when we would have gotten the illegal people, if they had successfully moved in, extricated from our house. A legal nightmare was averted. Since there was no burglar alarm, Charles inserted a camera in the front and back of the house and visited it more frequently.

More clients were shown the house and we were hopeful that it would soon be sold. Sure enough, we were eating dinner at a new restaurant on Saturday, February 5th, celebrating our wedding anniversary, when Charles received a phone call and email from an agent. We had received an offer to purchase the house, which we quickly discussed and agreed to accept. He responded back to the agent, and we were ecstatic! The house would now be sold. What a great night of celebration, first our anniversary, and then the sale of the house.

The next morning, we were preparing for our online worship service. Charles planned to go over to the house, just to make sure that everything was normal, and then stop by the landlord's office to pay the monthly rent for our church facility on his way home. However, "something" prevented him from going and we continued what was now our familiar online church service routine. After church, Charles told me that he was going to check on the house and pay the church rent. "Do you want to take a ride?" he asked me. "Sure," I said. We left and drove over to the house, still happy that we had a viable contract offer on it. As soon as we got there, we saw water going down the street. I asked Charles, "Why is there water running down the street from our driveway?" He immediately parked the car and told me to stay inside it. He went to inspect the perimeter of the house and, upon returning to the car, called the police. Someone had broken in yet again, and this time it was really bad.

The police came. The thief or thieves had stolen the copper pipes located in the basement, which had caused the basement to flood. Criminals will steal copper from vacant homes and buildings to sell it to scrap yards or other thieves on the street.

Although they do not make a lot of money from the copper of a single home, they can cause the homeowner thousands of dollars to repair the damage. In our case, the police quickly called the fire department, who quickly responded and were able to shut off the water. Unfortunately, there was quite a lot of damage in the basement. Although Charles was so very angry, he did not rant, go into a rage, nor use any profanity. He maintained his dignity, and I really respected his Christian witness. It would have been understandable for anyone to "lose it," given the situation at hand.

Charles contacted the company that did some of the renovations and thankfully, repairs began that Monday morning. He also contacted the real estate agent of the client who had submitted the contract to buy the house. Charles informed him that someone had broken into the house and that he would need a few days to correct the damage. The agent said that he understood, and that the house inspection could be delayed until that Friday. Miraculously, everything in the allotted time was replaced and/or repaired. The house looked beautiful again and passed inspection. It was really a miracle!

Despite the evil that had occurred, we saw how God had blessed us. Charles had planned to go check on the house that Sunday morning. According to the time stamp on the camera that he had placed at the front of the house, the perpetrator left through the front door at 8:00 a.m. If "something" had not stopped Charles that Sunday morning, he would have walked in on the crime, and we have no idea how devastating that could have been. Someone could have been injured or killed. Charles was really flabbergasted that during its recording, the video camera had apparently slipped down from its original positioning. Unbelievably, you could *not* see the face of the criminal. You could see only his body from the neck down. You could even see that he was carrying copper pipes out of the house. Initially, Charles was fuming, but we knew that God had not intended for us to see the man's face. It reminded us of what

Lawrence Johnson had said months earlier, that God did not intend for us to be on the road. God did not want us to see the criminal's face. If we had spotted someone who looked like the criminal in the video, we would have called the police. It would have been very nerve wracking and problematic. We could see God's hand at work in this situation.

Yes, we had a contract on the house, but we knew that the property was a risk for us until it was sold. So once the repairs began until the day of the closing, Charles stayed at the house, day and night. It was stressful and he had to stay there for weeks. He slept on an air mattress, and I carried prepared food to him. Ms. Joanne, one of our church members, also treated him to dinner on Friday evenings. Jasmine, Jessica and I would bring him breakfast on Sunday mornings, which was only one of the two meals of the week we had together. Minister Harley and his wife Jonniece, from their house, wonderfully conducted the broadcast of our online church services. Through the wonders of technology, Pastor Gray was able to join the live broadcast and deliver his sermons via cell phone.

God kept him safe, and no one broke into the house again. Five weeks later, the house closing took place, and our ordeal was finally over! The following week, we were able to make the trip to the Hampton University Choir Reunion. Remember, it was cancelled in 2020 but thankfully, rescheduled. We could now enjoy being together as a family. The stress we had endured was finally over! Thank God! We had dealt with two scenarios that many homeowners selling houses experience, and both situations could have produced horrific outcomes. God did indeed bless us and protect us!

Summer came quickly. Despite a couple of health challenges, we continued to prevail and enjoy God's blessings! On July 4th, we participated in an awesome evangelical ministry event, called *FreedomFest*, on the National Mall. Pastor Gray delivered a short message, Jasmine, Jessica and Ms. Joanne praise-danced, and I sang several gospel songs. It was wonderful! Later, we enjoyed a vacation in Virginia, a family reunion at the end of July, and near the end of August, our church fellowship's baptism on the Potomac River in Hague, Virginia. The weather prediction for the morning of the baptism was dire, and I even wondered if we should cancel it, but God prevailed! Instead of receiving the predicted severe storm, the Lord blessed us with a simply beautiful day embellished with sunshine, blue sky, and a wonderful beach. Most of all, a young man was baptized, publicly acknowledging his commitment to the Lord! We also celebrated Jasmine and Jessica's birthdays.

Life is good and God is great! In Matthew, Chapter 6, Verse 13, part of the verse reads, "...deliver us from evil." God did just that! Despite the evil and the trials we had endured earlier in the year, we were now able to relax and enjoy life. Little did we anticipate that unexpected grief was lurking right around the corner.

Chapter 21

BLESSINGS THROUGH GRIEF

"Mom, I have cancer!" These words, spoken by Geoffrey, shook me to my very core. How in the world was this happening? To begin with, for the past several years, we have conducted a telephone prayer meeting every day, Monday through Saturday. Unfortunately, this year, several of our participants encountered significant health challenges. One of these special prayer warriors, Ms. Holley (aka Sister Grace), became quite sick. For a brief period of time, she seemed to improve. However, she declined again. The Lord blessed her because her family knew that her probable end was near, which gave them time to visit her. She lived very near where Aunt Woncey had lived at Mapleshade, and they had been friends for many years. We soon got the news that Sister Grace finally wanted to go to the hospital. At about that time, Pastor Gray and I had gone down to Hague, Virginia, for some R&R (rest and relaxation). Hague is about forty-five minutes away from where she was hospitalized so we decided to visit her the morning after our arrival.

Simultaneously, Geoffrey was having what would soon be determined to be a <u>serious</u> health issue. For weeks, he thought that he had either become allergic to something or might be reacting to the possibility of mold in the North Carolina house he was renting. He experienced persistent itching all over his body. He was also fatigued and had lost weight but attributed it to working three jobs. By late September into early October, things got much worse. Through tests at his house and a chest x-ray orchestrated by an allergist, mold was ruled out as the cause of his symptoms. However, the x-ray did reveal a mass of tissue. After subsequent tests, it was determined that our 34-year-old son had cancer. We walked around, literally, in a state of shock—and grief.

The day we found out the devastating news about Geoffrey was the same day that our beloved Sister Grace began transitioning. Instead of visiting her as planned, her granddaughter called from the hospital to let us know that she had gone to be with the Lord. Pastor Gray and I went to her house to console the family, and simultaneously hid the shock and grief we were experiencing with Geoffrey's diagnosis.

I now had to go and see our son. I needed to hug him and simply be there for him. His father Greg and stepmother Denise live in South Carolina, about an hour away from Geoffrey. Fortunately, he was now staying with them. They were able to take him to medical appointments, make certain that he ate properly, and supply whatever else he needed.

Unfortunately, the news continued to get worse and Geoffrey's last test, a biopsy, confirmed that he had Hodgkin's Lymphoma, stage four. The cancer was located in three parts of his body. Lord have mercy! This was unreal! Once Geoffrey told my brother Larry about the x-ray results, Larry immediately got involved and assisted in making sure that Geoffrey's tests were accomplished quickly! I made hotel reservations and was thankful that I would finally see my son. Charles would stay in Maryland with Jasmine and Jessica.

On Tuesday, October 11, 2022, I rode down to South Carolina with Denise. She had driven up to Northern Virginia to attend her brother's memorial service. Greg stayed at their home with Geoffrey. The timing was perfect, and she welcomed my company. She had loved Geoffrey for many years, and it was a blessing that he was now staying with her and Greg. I spent a week in North Carolina, which was only a short distance away from them. I was so glad I was there. It was shocking to see how much weight Geoffrey had lost! For months, the cancer had caused the itching, depriving him of restful sleep. Seeing him scratching due to itching sensation was upsetting to witness. That Friday, Greg and I went with him to meet with the oncologist (a doctor who diagnoses/treats cancer), Dr. Asija. I could sense that she was very kind, professional, and caring. She verified the diagnosis and plan of action, which almost broke my heart. Larry participated via video phone call and concurred with her suggested method of treatment. Geoffrey would now begin chemotherapy two weeks later. Unbelievable! I was determined not to cry in his presence, and God gave me the strength to be strong.

Geoffrey and I spent some wonderful time together. It was such a blessing to be with him, and a part of me hated to leave him. He assured me that it was okay for me to go home and that we would get through this. Although I was torn whether to stay or leave, I complied with his sentiments. So after my week there, I caught a flight and headed home.

The cancer and chemo treatments have been the most difficult circumstances our son has ever experienced. The treatments last for hours, and the side effects have been horrific. By the time his body gets through most of the pain, sickness and fatigue, it is time to receive another treatment. One major blessing is that the itching finally stopped. Geoffrey has survived and continues to improve. He has been surrounded by a lot of love and his Costco work family has been very supportive. I will always be grateful to Geoffrey's supervisor, as he was the one who suggested to Geoffrey that his house be tested for mold. That really led to the allergist ordering the x-ray, which revealed the actual medical problem.

This part of our journey has been extremely difficult for our family to absorb. So many things have happened and many of them have been pregnant with grief. The local and national news report numerous stories of people being violently killed. We have also had family and church members affected by acts of violence and subsequent grief. I have found myself frequently crying while watching news reports and asking myself, "Why?" I realized that I was experiencing my own grief as Geoffrey's mother. How I wish I could have taken his place and endured his suffering. Each news story, each death, has impacted me deeply. I became even more sensitive to the grief that others around me were experiencing.

But God! Through this portion of our journey, I know that the Lord has been with us. Not only that, but He has communicated to me that Geoffrey will be fine. How? He called me on my cell phone. I know you might say, "What...how is that possible?" Well, the first call was on that Tuesday night en route to South Carolina. As Denise and I were traveling, my phone rang. It was my cousin, Arnell, who is also a minister. We rarely call one another, so her phone call came as a surprise. She told me that God had told her to call me and that He was going to perform something supernatural for us. I was stunned, especially because she knew nothing about what was going on with Geoffrey. Very few people at that time knew that anything was wrong. When I told her what was happening, she "spoke peace" to our situation, prayed for Geoffrey, and gave a few words to encourage me. After our call, I told Denise what had just happened, and that God had indeed orchestrated this phone call. We both acknowledged God's timing and His love, as He had let me know that it would be well with our son.

Every other Tuesday, Geoffrey endures the chemo and I ache for him. Charles reminds me of the Lord's promises, and we pray for our son every day. Yes, I have faith in God's healing. But as a mother, it greatly affects me; yes, it hurts me, deeply. But God is so loving. The Tuesday prior to Thanksgiving, a chemo day, I was being "affected" and as the tears fell from my face, the phone rang. I did not recognize the number and almost did not answer the call. "Something" made me answer it and I heard this very happy sounding voice on the other end of the call. This voice was that of the mother of one of my former choir members from a long time ago, and we had not spoken to one another in years. By the background noises, I could tell that she was in her car.

She told me that God had put me on her mind to call me and yet again, as was the case with Arnell, she knew nothing about Geoffrey's condition. When I told her, she proceeded to pray for Geoffrey, myself, and our family. It was such a blessing!

God was again reminding me, in His loving way, that He is in control. What a comfort it is to remember that the Creator of the universe continues to communicate with His children. Through my conversation with her, I smiled through my tears. After her call, I felt better, and I thanked the Lord for taking the time to call me, yet again! Most of all, I thanked Him for His love, compassion, and His blessings. I knew that throughout the remainder of this journey, more blessings would come!

CONCLUSION

Within each chapter, I hope that you have experienced a sense of our incredible journey, sustained by a wonderful God—His blessings, His protection, and most of all, His Love. Lovingly, sometimes God will use other people and/or situations to bless and protect you. Other times, He may speak to your mind, and you will hear a "little voice" telling you something. Yes, we know that little voice... the one that sometimes we obey, yet sometimes ignore. You read in my accounts that I sometimes heard the little voice and how my obedience to its directions allowed me to receive unbelievable blessings. Jesus said in John 10:27, "My sheep hear my voice, and I know them, and they follow me." As I reflect on my life, I know there were times that I, myself, did not obey the little voice, which would almost always produce negative results. What's interesting is that He speaks to me very succinctly. Since I am a "wordy" person, I have learned to differentiate between my thoughts and His voice. I don't always get this right because I am still a "work in progress"!

Remember that we are living in perilous times with dangers seen and unseen, including the threat of unforeseen viruses, diseases, and mass shootings. Now, more than ever, as we navigate through these challenges, we need to be in communication with the One who hung the stars in the sky. It is not about religion. It is about "relationship," a personal relationship with the Lord! Hearing His voice is so very critical. The night I could have wound up at the bottom of the elevator shaft still haunts me. Yet it is so humbling and reminds me of the depth of God's love.

As our journey continues, we must pursue making plans for our daughters' futures. Who will take care of them once Charles and I have departed this world? Our pursuit for the solution was temporarily tabled, as Geoffrey's diagnosis propelled us in an unexpected direction. As we have continued to manage the challenges of everyday life, our primary focus has been to support our son in any way we could. Although we as parents have felt some of his pain, we can only imagine what he has truly gone through. We know that God understands, as Christ took our place on the cross. He understands, even better than I, Geoffrey's pain and suffering, as is experienced by so many others. We have had no choice but to trust God that Geoffrey would be healed. Amazingly, writing this book strengthened me for our son's cancer journey. Many people have prayed for him, and we are indeed grateful. He has told me that he has felt our prayers as we have continued to stand on the prevailing word of God.

As I concluded this writing, the Lord blessed us yet again! Five weeks after the conclusion of chemotherapy, Geoffrey received the long-awaited Pet Scan. In fact, he stated that the date of the scan would be his "new" birthday, as he anticipated a positive outcome. Anyway, he chose not to look at the results in his medical patient portal and decided to wait to find out the status at his upcoming oncology appointment the following Tuesday. The day after the scan, I participated at Sargent Church for the funeral of Letricia's (one of my choir members) mother. The choir had been asked to sing and I conducted them, which was actually the first time that the choir sang together since the onset of the pandemic. It was a blessing to be a part of this wonderful lady's tribute. She was very special to everyone and once even babysat our daughters when they were infants.

After the service, I was sitting in our van in the church's parking lot, ready to leave. Upon looking at my phone, I realized I had missed a call from Geoffrey. I called him...he was crying. "Mom, I'm cancer free!" His oncologist's nurse had called him, and hearing those words, I "lost it"! I literally broke down and proceeded, like Geoffrey, to cry tears of joy! After our conversation, I called in to our church fellowship's daily prayer line and proclaimed the "cancer free" announcement. Geoffrey had already reached Charles, who heads the prayer group that had been praying for our son since his diagnosis. We all proceeded to exclaim our thanks to God! After the prayer call, although I had planned to leave to go on an errand, I decided to go back inside the church and share the news with everyone at the repast. Shouts of joy and hugs erupted! Charles was down in Hague, Virginia, working at the house, so I couldn't hug him at that moment. Yet this was the next best thing, being with people who loved Geoffrey, some having known him his entire life, a church family who had been praying, supporting, and communicating with him through this challenging ordeal. What a blessing!!

I called Larry to thank him for all his support, only to find out that Geoffrey had already called him. Larry, of course, was elated and shared with me something very special. I knew that prior to his retirement, for many of his years with several pharmaceutical companies, he had held high-level positions responsible for "drug safety." What I didn't know was that the biological therapy Geoffrey received to raise his blood counts after chemo was one of the therapies that Larry oversaw. Little did he know that his expertise and dedication to safety would someday benefit his only nephew!

Now, a short time later, on my way to my errand, my cell phone rang. The name that flashed up on my call screen said Karen. Not immediately recognizing the name, I asked myself, "Who is this?" Believe it or not, Karen is the lady who called me in November, as I was having an emotional moment, knowing that Geoffrey was suffering through chemo that day. We had not spoken since. And now, she did not know I had indeed been crying yet again; but this time, my tears were those of JOY!! When I told her about Geoffrey's latest development, and how I had been periodically crying for the last two hours, I heard silence. She and I began to praise God, as we both knew that the Lord had her call again at this appointed time! Not only did Karen bless me, but she stated that my words to her had now encouraged her also. Overall, it was as if the Lord was yet reminding me, and all of us, that He had promised Geoffrey's healing. He was reminding us of the importance of faith and most of all, His magnificent love!

Recently, the Lord recalled to my mind a situation from many years ago, the day our family van was stolen. My children and I had arrived home and gone inside. Within minutes, I heard a sound from the gravel parking area in front of our house. This sound normally meant that someone was either parking a vehicle or leaving in one. When I looked out the window, the van was gone. It was so brazen, as whomever committed the crime, did so in broad daylight! Our van was found several days later, and the insurance company determined that it was beyond repair. We went to salvage whatever personal items could be removed and were emotionally repulsed by the conditions inside the vehicle. It was heart wrenching. The criminals had destroyed virtually everything in sight; they even broke up the girls' crayons, which Jasmine and Jessica used to often color with, especially during long travel trips. When we searched through the vehicle to make certain that there was nothing left of value, we spotted a thick paperback book. Upon turning it over, we realized it was the Bible that Charles' mother had given to Geoffrey. Miraculously, it was the only thing in the van that was not destroyed, and it was completely intact. I remember giving it back to Geoffrey later that day, telling him that regardless of the evil or devastation around us, the Word of God would always prevail. It reveals God's promises to us and I have learned, over time, to read, trust and believe it!

As I penned this book, I relived so many memories. Only God could have helped me remember astonishing things that I know were His divine blessings. Many of you may categorize them as supernatural, and I agree with your assessment. Some might read about our blessings cited in this book and simply theorize that they were only coincidences. Others might even believe that we were just "lucky." You are all entitled to your beliefs but for me, I know that God showed us His power, time and time again.

When I remember how God used strangers to convey messages to Charles and myself, how He orchestrated the girls attending the Ivymount School, how He prepared them for 911, how He directed me to Starbucks to meet the transportation supervisor, how he prevented me from death by car accidents so many times, and again, how He prevented me from stepping into the elevator that night... I think about these events and still find myself in awe. I also believe that if you, who have read this book, sit for a moment and reflect on your life, you will remember the blessings you have received as you have persevered through your own journey!

For those of you who make up the special needs community, including those who serve us in your professions and volunteer endeavors, stay encouraged. You are indeed an inspiration to us all!

Now for those of you with special needs children who ride, have ridden, or will ride the "little yellow school bus," I hope that this book has encouraged you. Many times, you may have felt that God does not care about your situation. Some of you may have felt that you did something wrong during your lives to cause whatever situation you are in. That thinking is very wrong! In fact, there is an excellent example of that in the Bible. John 9:1-3 says: "And as Jesus passed by, he saw a man who was blind from his birth. And his disciples asked him, saying, 'Rabbi, who sinned, this man or his parents, that he was born blind?' Jesus answered, neither this man nor his parents, but that the works of God should be revealed in him." Jasmine and Jessica are the most loving and "happy" people that we know! God's works continue to be revealed within both of them and they bless our lives every day.

Some of you may feel that God has dealt you an awful hand and you do not deserve to go through what you are going through. I feel for you, but once sin entered the world, sickness accompanied it. Trust me, the Lord understands your feelings, but He knows that you can make it and take care of your children. Most of all, He wants you to depend on Him. Matthew 19:26 says: "Jesus looked at them and said, 'With man this is impossible, but with God all things are possible.'" God will give you the strength to help your children excel and become a blessing to others. Your children all have talents and gifts. Regardless of their status, they are all precious in the sight of God. Our daughters have in their own special ways, made Charles and I better people, better parents, and stronger Christians. I pray that you never give up on God nor these special children. In the Old Testament of the Bible, one scripture, Deuteronomy 31:6, reminds us that, "He will not fail you, nor forsake you." Remember also, that YOU will also bless others as they progress through their journeys.

If you need help, reach out to others. Your family, friends, church family and others can help you. To everyone, regardless of your circumstances, involving special needs children or otherwise, please don't isolate yourselves! There are support groups and other organizations that can assist you. In fact, a few years after the girls were born, I realized the importance of sharing with other special needs parents/guardians and started a lunchtime support group at my agency. It was great to be with others to exchange knowledge and experiences!

Whatever you are experiencing, special needs or otherwise, there are times you may cry, feel exhausted, or sometimes wonder if you will survive. But please continue to trust and believe. God did not provide the blessings I have cited in this book because we were "good people." He did all He did because He loves us, and we have a personal relationship with Him. Psalm 115:12 says, "The LORD has been mindful of us; He will bless us."

Some years ago, I asked the Lord why He used Jasmine and Jessica's challenges to reveal Himself to me. The little voice in my mind said something that I will never forget: "That's where your focus is." That response was incredible but also very thought-provoking. Yes, with my attention on the girls, it was much more obvious to see God orchestrating, guiding, protecting, and blessing us. Yet my main focus should be on the Lord! My prayer is that all of you will embrace and grow in your relationship with Him. To those of you whose life has a different journey other than special needs, my advice is the same. I pray that you will have faith and trust in God. I pray that you will take the words to heart that my dad used to say, "May we love Him better and may we serve Him better."

So remember to trust in the Lord, pray, and take care of yourselves, including your own health and spiritual well-being. Try to read the Bible daily, as God's word will strengthen you! All of us are on a journey, and we all need the blessings of our Heavenly Father.

I pray that this book has inspired and encouraged you. As my husband says at the end of our church fellowship's daily prayer time, "Be encouraged, God is on our side." Yes, He always has been, is, and always will be. May your journey, today and always, be blessed by His love!

A Few Journey Memories

Dad Lawrence and Mom Bertha

Aunt Woncey and Uncle T.W.

Jessica, Mom Pauline and Jasmine

Jasmine and Jessica's 21st Birthday With Ivymount Friends

Jessica and Jasmine At An Epic Christmas Event

Jasmine and Jessica With Henrietta and Gary

Jasmine and Jessica With Family

Our Family on a Mother's Day

A Birthday Celebration
Arie, Pam, Larry and Rosetta

A Birthday Celebration
Carolyn and Bernard

**Pastor Gray, Geoffrey, and
SOTCC Praise Dancers
(Ms. Joanne, Jasmine and Jessica)**

Our 25th Wedding Anniversary

About the Author

Arie Gray was born in Portsmouth, Virginia, as Arie Dell Johnson. She spent much of her childhood in St. Louis, Missouri, and since 1968, has resided in Maryland. She graduated from Central High School in Seat Pleasant, Maryland.

In 1977, Arie received a Bachelor of Science degree in Music Education from Hampton Institute (now Hampton University) and in 1983, a master's degree in library science from the University of Maryland. During the beginning of her career, she taught music education in Prince Georges County for four years and then worked as a Reader's Advisor for the Martin Luther King Memorial Library in Washington DC. One year later, she was hired by the Defense Intelligence Agency (DIA), where she spent the remainder of her career as a computer instructor. She joined the Alpha Kappa Alpha Sorority and also became the female vocalist for the Ambition Band which performed R&B music in the Washington DC area. Arie has been a choir director at several churches and for many years, co-directed the Sargent Gospel-Aires Choir. She is now retired but continues to conduct the music ministry at her church, Spirit Of Truth Christian Church. Currently, Arie is an active member of the Northern Virginia Ministers' Wives and Widows organization.

In addition to being a choir director, Arie has been keyboardist, singer, and composer for decades. She is also a gospel recording artist and recorded a CD named "Miracle of Love", named after one of her compositions. She attributes her spiritual growth to her late uncle, Dr. T. W. Morris and her husband, Pastor Charles S. Gray. Arie and Charles are the proud parents of Geoffrey Spriggs and twins - Jasmine and Jessica Gray.

Made in the USA
Coppell, TX
25 July 2023

19574344R00118